Eugene Onegin
A Novel in Verse

by Alexander Sergeevich Pushkin

• • •

A Novel Versification

by Douglas Hofstadter

Eugene Onegin

A Novel in Verse

by Alexander Sergeevich Pushkin

• • • ● • • •

A Novel Versification

by Douglas Hofstadter

• ● •

*With sketches by Achille Varzi
and chapter heads by the translator*

•

Basic Books
A Member of the Perseus Books Group

Published by Basic Books, A Member of the Perseus Books Group.

Design and composition by the translator, using FullWrite 2. Cover art and sketches by Achille Varzi; chapter heads by the translator.

Library of Congress Cataloguing-in-Publication Data

Pushkin, Alexander Sergeevich (1799–1837).
 [Евгений Онегин. Evgeniĭ Onegin. English]
Eugene Onegin: a novel in verse / Alexander Pushkin;
 translated, with a preface and notes, by Douglas
 Hofstadter.
Includes bibliographical references.
ISBN 0-465-02094-1
I. Hofstadter, Douglas R. (1945–   ) II. Title.

00 01 02 RRD 9 8 7 6 5 4 3 2 1

•

Not aiming to amuse the folk in
Nabókov's *monde,* but just my friends,
I'd hoped to tender you a token,
Dear Falens, worthier of the blends
That make your souls so rich and precious,
So rife with sacred dreams, and with
Poetic lines that e'er refresh us,
And lofty thoughts, and charm and pith;
Oh, well... Take what will henceforth mesh us:
This suite of chapters, one through eight —
Half-droll, half-sad, sometimes romantic,
But down-to-earth and ne'er pedantic,
The careless fruit I've born of late —
The tossing, turning inspirations
From greener and from grayer years:
My mind's chilled white-wine decantations,
My heart's red wines, distilled from tears.

•

Table of Contents

•

•

Translator's Preface

Six Words Go Out, Six Others Come Back

MY UNCLEar, awkward, ski-jump start will, in the end, be resolved and cleared up, and will (I can hope!) even coax a quick smile. But for now, well… Onward, onward, speeds my story — a strange one, perhaps, but then, so are many.

We may as well begin on a blustery October eve, as my stalwart buddy Greg Huber and I are trudging westward, straight into the biting wind, along Saint Petersburg's Petrovskaya Embankment; with us is a young Russian acquaintance, Natasha, a friend of a friend of Greg's, whom we've met only once before. She is about 21, bright, open, and pretty, and has told us she teaches English to children in a small school in town. As we walk, with the sun still bouncing a few feeble rays off clouds in the west, night seems reluctant to take over from the purplish dusk. All three of us suddenly shiver as a specially sharp gust comes whipping through, and I turn to Natasha and utter a few words that have just popped into my head: *Vot séver, túchi nagonyáya, dokhnúl, zavýl* ("Here's the north, clouds a-chasing; it blew, it howled"). She flicks me a little smile and throws in a few words of her own: *I vot samá idyót volshébnitsa zimá* ("And here comes winter herself, the sorceress").

I'm pleased, but this is a mundane event, so mundane that I let it pass without a word. We cross the Troitskii Bridge, turn right, pass the imposing Admiralty, find our restaurant as night settles, and at dinner talk, laugh, talk. But for some reason, over the next few days, this symmetric little exchange — six words sent out, six words received — keeps reverberating in my mind, and slowly it dawns on me that what transpired that blustery purple evening — and precisely *because* it was so ordinary, so mundane — was in fact an extraordinary, magical event, filled with hidden meaning.

The words I had spoken, though they'd popped spontaneously into my head at that moment, were not of my own invention: my command of Russian is, so sad to say, not nearly that good. They were lifted from a sonnet written by Alexander Pushkin in the late 1820's — line 12 and half of line 13 of the sonnet, to be specific. Nor were Natasha's words invented by her, for they were the remainder of line 13, plus the sonnet's concluding line. Here are those lines, as they appear in the poem:

> Вот север, тучи нагоняя,
> Дохнул, завыл — и вот сама
> Идёт волшебница зима.

And so Natasha and I had swapped successive pieces of a poem with each other. That's cute, but what's so extraordinary in it? Indeed, the truth of the matter is that when I threw my six words at her, I was almost *expecting* something of the sort. What I was thinking was roughly this: "Russians know their Pushkin; here's a snippet of Pushkin that describes this scene right now; she'll of course recognize these words, and she'll like the fact that an American knows them." And my hunch was right; accordingly, I was not astonished, just pleased, whence the lack of comment.

What was it, then, that made my perception of this event flip so dramatically? In a word, it was its sheer randomness. Firstly, my six-word phrase was by no means the Russian counterpart of a famous opening nugget like "To be or not to be" or "Fourscore and seven years ago" — it lies buried inside the fairly arbitrary stanza 29 of Chapter VII of Pushkin's eight-chapter novel in verse *Eugene Onegin,* which consists of nearly 400 stanzas, almost all of them tetrameter sonnets in the purest of iambic meter. Secondly, Natasha was not a literary scholar, or even a student of Russian literature — she was a fairly typical product of the modern Russian educational system. And yet out of some 5,300 lines of *Eugene Onegin,* she had instantly and effortlessly recognized my few words — but not just that, without even blinking, she had instantly and effortlessly completed the stanza.

I knew well, from prior conversations with Russian friends, that many Russians know a great deal of *Eugene Onegin* by heart, and people had occasionally said to me, "I used to know it all, when I was in high school." At first I had been incredulous, and thought they must be pulling my leg. Even when I realized they were not joking, I was skeptical. How could anyone memorize 5,300 lines of poetry? I myself had never memorized more than about 100 lines of poetry — a long speech by Cyrano in Edmond Rostand's drama in verse *Cyrano de Bergerac,* when I was in high school — and doing that had felt like a huge *tour de force* to me.

Nonetheless, having heard so many similar claims, I had slowly come to believe that educated Russians were very familiar with a lot of this novel, and that's why I confidently quoted a few lines to Natasha. She, in turn, had confirmed my expectations. But what she did with such ease really made the Russian love for Pushkin's novel hit home, because the stanza I had quoted is neither central nor celebrated — it does not stand out from the whole in any way. In effect, I had closed my eyes, thrown a dart at the novel, and hit it in a random line, and then, without my intending it as such, that line had played the role of a spot-check of her knowledge, which she passed with flying colors. And in a certain sense, Natasha herself had been selected from the Russian population by the throw of another dart. The upshot was that a tiny exchange of twelve words constituted an amazing demonstration of just how profoundly Alexander Pushkin's novel in verse pervades the minds of his compatriots nearly 170 years after its completion.

An Opera or a Novel?

When, sometime in my dim past, I first heard the words "Eugene Onegin", it was as the title of a Tchaikovsky opera. The name "Alexander Pushkin" was nowhere in sight, nor was the idea of poetry. And in recent years I have found, over and over again, that my experience is pretty typical, outside of Russia. To the

Translator's Preface

average culturally-inclined adult in a western land such as ours, the two words "Eugene Onegin" (properly pronounced, by the way, "Onn-*yay*-ghin", so as to rhyme, approximately, with "Ron Reagan") tend to bring to mind an opera but little else, while the name "Pushkin" coaxes up a vaguish image of some nineteenth-century literary figure but seldom any specific work.

In Russia, by contrast, Pushkin is a universal hero — not the musty equivalent of Wordsworth or Longfellow, nor even of the bright star of Shakespeare; Pushkin is much closer to the common people than any of those. He is seen as the founder of Russian literature, as the prototypical symbol of Russia's cultural greatness, and as a vivid and lovable though flawed human being. To speak Pushkin's name is to evoke an aura inseparable from the beauty of the Russian language. Even nonintellectuals revere him and know some of his poems by heart. The closest counterpart that I can come up with is the role played by Frédéric Chopin in the hearts of Poles.

Of all of Pushkin's output, which is sizable despite his death in a senseless duel at 37, the most revered is without question this novel, *Eugene Onegin*. Although we outside of Russia tend to think of Dostoevsky's *Crime and Punishment* or Tolstoy's *War and Peace* as the top icons of Russian literature, within Russia *Eugene Onegin* knows no rival. Wherefore, then, the relatively low level of appreciation abroad? It's hard to say for sure, but one factor must be that *Eugene Onegin,* being as it is in verse, is considerably harder to translate into other languages than most novels are. Another factor might be the work's compactness — it is very slender. Perhaps another quality that makes this poetic novel seem strange or, well, *foreign* to some readers is its unprecedented manner of intermingling lightness and seriousness — that is, its uniquely contrapuntal character, on which I'll now say a little.

Those who have seen the Tchaikovsky opera will remember it as a lugubrious story of star-crossed lovers, of anger, jealousy, and tragic death. And yet, although that is indeed the "plot line" of the novel, it is but one facet of the work. What makes Pushkin's book so marvelously alluring is not its sad plot line (which is fine as far as it goes), but the way in which that line, like a single line in a piece by Bach, weaves its way in and out of the focus, yielding the floor to other lines of quite different character.

Above all, the novel's counterpoint involves an intricate, unpredictable bouncing back and forth between the characters in the story and Pushkin's own droll, sardonic observations about life, about himself, about poetry, about women's legs, about friendship, about wine, about truncated lives, about nature, about each of the seasons, about foreign words used in Russian, about hypocrisy, and on and on. All of this is executed in graceful, sparkling, yet mostly colloquial language that is nearly always pellucid to a native speaker of Russian, even today. Altogether, reading *Eugene Onegin* provides as tingling and keen a jolt to the lively mind as the stark Finnish habit of jumping back and forth between sauna and snowbank does to the healthy body.

Tchaikovsky's opera, whatever its merits as drama or music might be, conveys little if any of this exquisite polyphonic charm, since voices other than the plot are totally lacking. Moreover, despite the fact that many stanzas from the original poem have been set to music, the linguistic charm is also largely missing. For nonspeakers of Russian, the reason is, of course, that the poetry is completely inaudible as such, even on a phonetic level — but this lack extends also to native speakers, oddly enough. It is hard to hear the arias' lyrics as verse, in part because, as any opera-goer knows, words, even when sung in one's own language, are often hard to make out, and in part because the natural poetic beat is overridden by the musical beat. And so... with the polyphony missing and the poetry missing, the opera is but the feeblest, faintest trace of the novel.

For the opera to have supplanted its sparkling source, in the eyes of the non-Russian world, as the chief referent of the term "Eugene Onegin" is, in my opinion, a sad development, and for that reason, I must say, it would be a source of great pleasure to me if the appearance of my "novel versification" of Pushkin's novel in verse in 1999, the poet's bicentennial year, contributed in some way to the reversal of this trend, and helped to restore the place of honor to *Eugene Onegin* the novel, as opposed to *Eugene Onegin* the opera.

A Nonspeaker of Russian Encounters *Eugene Onegin*

It will not have escaped notice of readers of this preface that on its first page, I commented that my spoken Russian is rather poor. How in the world, then, could I have even considered getting involved in such a project, let alone have had the hubris to think I could do a decent job of it? A good question, and the story is, I think, of some interest.

In 1986, I read the novel *The Golden Gate* by Vikram Seth, and was bowled over by its lilt and grace, as well as its plot and characterizations. Never had I imagined a novel in verse, and Seth's work impressed me enormously. I so much enjoyed it, in fact, that I wrote a letter to Seth and suggested we get together next time I was in his neck of the woods. Not too many weeks passed before we were sharing a leisurely Californian coffee, and in the course of our chat he pointed out something that somehow had failed to register on me in my first reading — namely, three stanzas in his Chapter 5 that explicitly declare that his inspiration had been British diplomat Charles Johnston's "luminous translation" into English of Pushkin's novel in verse. This was an eye-opener for me. I knew next to nothing about Pushkin or his works, but Seth, in a generous gesture, bought me a copy of the Johnston version of *Onegin*, and in so doing opened wide a gate through which I might easily pass into the golden land of Pushkin. And yet, though I peered through it, I did not walk through Seth's golden gate. Instead, I left Johnston sitting on my bookshelf for five or six years, utterly uncracked.

Then one day in late 1992, by lucky chance, I ran across another English *Onegin*, this one from the pen of James Falen, professor of Russian at the University of Tennessee. I riffled through it, and since, at least on the surface, it looked as if it wasn't half-bad, I purchased it, more or less on a whim. Soon Falen's version was sitting right next to Johnston's on my dusty shelf, both of them now relegated to the same sad literary limbo.

But as the weeks passed, the lonely pair beckoned and nagged at me, and one day in the spring of 1993, knowing how my wife Carol and I got a kick out of reading to each other, I pulled them down and asked Carol what she thought of the idea of our reading them *both* out loud together. She was game, and thus began a little evening ritual in which, our children having been duly storied and cuddled and now drifting off into golden dreams, we would climb into our own bed, plump our pillows till they were right, and then plunge into our double-barreled *Onegin*. One of us would read a Falen stanza, then the other would read the "same" Johnston stanza, then we'd comment on them, after which we'd read the same stanzas out loud once more, make more comments, then move on to the next stanza.

In this plodding but pleasing manner, Carol and I got to know both translators' styles, got to know the structure and characters of *Eugene Onegin*, and got to know something of Alexander Pushkin, to boot. We even felt we could get a slight taste of the Russian poetry itself, for between the two translators' ways of phrasing things, details of the original in a certain sense showed through. Although we were impressed by both translators, we soon came to the mutual conclusion that Falen's translation, despite Seth's lavish praise for Johnston, was smoother, more graceful, and far clearer.

Some two years later — a nightmare period during which, out of the blue, Carol succumbed to an unsuspected brain cancer and our small family was turned upside down by the loss — I was slowly trying to regain some vague semblance of normalcy, and I recalled one special, though now most poignant, source of sanity: the joy of reading *Onegin*. I wondered what other translations might exist and how they might sound, so I went to the library and got a hold of several. A few were pretty wretched, but two of them seemed decent — one by Walter Arndt, and the other by Oliver Elton, later revised by A. D. P. Briggs. I carefully perused both of them, comparing stanza after stanza with those by Falen and Johnston, and in this manner came to have a clear sense for all four verse translations still in print. I still liked Falen's the best, but saw virtues in all of them. And at that point, I wrote a comparative review of the four translations for *The New York Times*, which subsequently, and greatly expanded, became two chapters of my book *Le Ton beau de Marot*.

In the spring semester of 1997, just as *Le Ton beau de Marot* was about to appear, I offered a seminar on verse translation at Indiana University, and among the many works we were looking at, *Eugene Onegin* — in these four highly diverse anglicizations — featured prominently. I felt the best way to compare the four approaches was to ask each student to concentrate on one stanza, studying it carefully in all four translations, making notes about prominent merits or defects, and then coming to class and performing the four rival stanzas out loud with as much skill as they could muster, after which a class-wide discussion would take place. I decided to focus on Chapter III, and from it selected a section that included the most famous part of the novel — Tatyana's letter to Onegin. As a lark, I treated myself as a student along with the other dozen and, wearing that lowly hat, I was assigned by our demanding professor to discuss a series of twenty-five successive lines in the middle of Tatyana's letter (one of just three parts of the novel that are not in sonnet form).

As I was preparing my presentation, it occurred to me that my students, only one or two of whom knew any Russian, would probably benefit from hearing how at least a few lines sound in their original tongue, and so, having studied a little Russian some twenty-five years earlier, I got out my copy of the authentic text (which I had also purchased, just for fun) and sounded out the words in my portion very slowly. I found it rough going, and in quest of smoothness, I read this short section out loud to myself at least thirty times, and then contacted a Russian friend and asked her to critique me. It turned out I had a good long way to go in mastery of Russian phonetics, but Ariadna's careful coaching was of enormous help to me, and encouraged me to redouble my efforts at accuracy. And so I kept on reading my lines out loud over and over to myself, and after another thirty or forty readings, I realized they were getting pretty familiar. Of all things, could I perhaps *memorize* this stretch of Russian poetry? Well, why not? It seemed an odd thing to do, given my track record at poetry memorization, but it appealed to me.

Fascination Turns to Passion

How vividly I recalled a conversation in which Carol's and my old friend Marina had nonplussed us by nonchalantly remarking, "I used to know the whole book by heart — and so did many of my friends." In light of such heroic feats, it seemed to me only reasonable that I, too, should memorize at least a *little* of this novel. But how crazy, were I to follow that route, to be able to recite merely the middle third of Tatyana's letter! And so I bravely decided to expand my self-challenge to include all 79 lines of that celebrated epistle.

The long and the short of it is that within a couple of weeks, I finally got the whole letter under my belt, and my students were amused when I came to class and told them that that morning while in the shower, I'd repeated it to myself in eight minutes; then a couple of days later I proudly reported I'd got it down to four minutes; and the following week I finally attained my goal of three minutes. They thought my concern with speed was silly, but to me it was crucial that the lines flow extremely easily, which essentially required my being able to say them in my sleep.

Needless to say, all this was quite an odd twist in my growing involvement with *Eugene Onegin,* for heretofore I had dealt exclusively with various translations, while now I was dealing with the real McCoy. I decided that, as a kind of icing on the cake, I would also memorize the stanza that introduces Tatyana's letter, because it had always been a favorite. But truth to tell, I had lots of favorite stanzas, and so one little addition like this followed another, and pretty soon I had memorized stanzas scattered through all eight chapters, in total amounting to over twice the

Translator's Preface

length of Tatyana's letter. No doubt about it — I was hooked on this off-the-wall new mental sport.

Unfortunately, I was no great shakes at memorizing, and to get a stanza really ingrained in my memory so that I could recite it smoothly even when starting cold, I found I needed somewhere in the neighborhood of 300 to 400 mental rehearsals. To reach such large numbers, I found myself exploiting my twenty-minute showers, my three-mile runs, various and sundry car rides, plane rides, doctors' waiting rooms, children's soccer games, and so on — in short, any and every moment of spare time — in repeating one stanza or another to myself.

One of the weirder aspects of all this was that I was committing to memory dozens of lines in which one, two, or more words were completely novel to me. Although of course I looked each one up and knew its rough meaning, these words were nonetheless in some sense little more than rote sounds to me. But any time a word appeared in two or three different stanzas, in quite different contexts, it started picking up its own flavor and started being imbued with more of a true meaning. So through memorization, my vocabulary began growing, although not in anything like the order in which one acquires words in a class. Ironic though it seemed, here I was, cutting my Russian-language baby teeth on the most hallowed work of Russian literature!

In early September of 1997, six months or so into this odyssey, I had committed between thirty and forty stanzas to memory and was working on the first three stanzas of Chapter VII, which I found deeply moving, when one morning a friend happened to put on a recording of Ella Fitzgerald singing the melancholy song "Spring Is Here", by Rodgers and Hart. All at once, I was struck by a remarkable resonance between Pushkin's lines and Hart's lyrics, both in subject matter and in tone. Both poets were dealing with a spring whose return is anything but joyous, and I marveled at how an American popular song from the 1930's and some Russian sonnets from the 1820's could overlap so greatly.

Alone in the house that afternoon, I played the song again, and as Ella's mellifluous voice intoned the sad words in English, I recited stanzas VII.2 and VII.3 out loud in a deep, despairing voice, thus baldly superimposing male voice onto female, Russian poetry onto American song, the 1820's onto the 1930's, and "high culture" onto "pop culture". I found myself strangely moved by this stark juxtaposition, and as soon as the song was over, I played it again and recited the Pushkin again. I did this at least a dozen times before having to stop so I could pick up my kids at school.

That evening, so engrossed in those stanzas, I found myself wanting to "possess" them even more profoundly and personally, much as one wishes to possess a beloved as profoundly as possible, and the only more intimate kind of involvement I could imagine was to try translating them to my mother tongue — making them truly my own poetry. I still had no thought whatsoever of doing the whole book; I merely wanted to see if translating a few isolated stanzas was within my reach, or if I would make a fool of myself in trying. Although Falen's versions of these stanzas had touched me deeply when I'd read them, luckily his lines weren't so fresh in my mind as to crowd out my own ideas. This gave me hope that I wouldn't have to constantly check my lines to make sure that I wasn't unconsciously rewriting Falen. Thus, in a daring mood, I simply closed my eyes and took the plunge with VII.1.

I found that it took me a couple of hours to get a first draft, and then I spent two or three further hours just making small adjustments here and there, in order to polish the result ever more. And so the next day, I had an Onegin stanza of my very own — and then, two days later, *mirabile dictu*, I had all three at the start of Chapter VII. And yet, somehow, I still did not see the handwriting on the wall.

The Crystalline Building Blocks
of this Novel in Verse

Perhaps at this point an interlude is needed to explain the nature of the so-called "Onegin stanza", for without a crystal-clear understanding of its building blocks, one cannot fully appreciate the novel's artistry. Pushkin, influenced by Byron, decided to try his hand at writing a novel in verse, but he chose a very different structure in which to pack all his ideas. Basically, Pushkin's crystal vessel was a sonnet, but a very special form of sonnet. In the first place, each of its lines was composed in uncompromising iambic tetrameter — stresses falling always on even-numbered syllables. In the second place, all stanzas shared exactly the same rhyme scheme: ABAB, CCDD, EFFEGG. And thirdly — and this is the touch that, at least for me, really gives these stanzas their distinct flavor — he chose an elegant and catchy quasi-alternating pattern of *feminine* and *masculine* rhymes.

This distinction is not that well known in English, so I will explain it here. A masculine rhyme involves *one* stressed syllable at the end of each line, such as "turn" and "burn", whereas a feminine rhyme involves *two* syllables, the second of which is unstressed, as in "turning" and "burning". Note that in the example, the unstressed syllables, rather than rhyming with each other, are simply identical. Most feminine rhymes are that way: stressed syllables rhyme, unstressed syllables coincide. However, to my ear at least, it is also acceptable for the unstressed syllables to rhyme (an example of this sort that I use in Chapter VI is "rock's doze" and "cock's crows"). In any case, Pushkin decided that feminine rhymes would always occur on the A, C, and E lines of each stanza. Thus the fixed pattern of masculine lines and feminine lines is this: FMFM, FFMM, FMMFMM.

One of the effects of using feminine rhymes in iambic tetrameter is that each feminine line has nine syllables, all five of whose odd-numbered beats are unstressed, whereas masculine lines have just eight syllables, and just four unstressed beats. There is thus a slight metric irregularity to the Onegin stanza: 9898, 9988, 988988, to spell out the syllable-counts explicitly. This, to me, is the key to much of the charm of the Pushkinian crystal that pervades these pages.

Although my commas in the pattern "ABAB, CCDD, EFFEGG" seem to suggest that each stanza breaks up naturally into two quatrains and a sextet, this is not at all the case. Pushkin often expresses ideas that do not break cleanly at quatrain boundaries, nor indeed, even at line boundaries. There are even cases where a sentence will start near the end of one stanza and jump right across into the next stanza.

Many commentators have pointed out that the first twelve lines of the Onegin stanza neatly display all three possible rhyme patterns for a quatrain — namely, ABAB (interleaved), CCDD (separated), and EFFE (sandwich-style) — and they are then complemented by a closing couplet, GG. But though many stanzas do end in couplets that have a "zinger" quality to them, having a stand-alone couplet at the end is certainly not *de rigueur*, and indeed it would be most misleading to suggest that there is any fixed pattern at all of how semantic chunks are distributed among the fourteen lines. Quite to the contrary, Pushkin plays very free and easy with the flow of thoughts among his lines, and a great deal of the charm of his poetry emanates precisely from the manner in which unpredictability and irregularity coexist with an overarching, rigid formal structure.

The Handwriting on the Wall is Finally Seen

I'll pick up now on my personal saga. The memorizing continued apace throughout the fall of 1997, and several weeks later another stanza in Chapter VII took hold of me so strongly that I again felt the urge to try converting it to English. This time something utterly unexpected happened. I'd done what I thought was a fine job of anglicization and was admiring my own handiwork when my eye lit on a strange semi-pattern at the lines' beginnings: nine out of the fourteen capital letters were, for some odd reason, "T". I looked at those "T"'s and thought, "How curious! A pattern crying out for completion!"

Other people might perhaps not have reacted that way, but it seems to me that it's just a question of how one is tuned. Thus I find it hard to imagine *anyone* who, upon noticing that a sonnet just penned had all but *one* of its lines beginning with "T", would not feel at least a little tempted to try to make them *all* do so. What if all but *two* started with "T"? All but three? All but five? Different people will have different thresholds, and mine might be lower than some, but I daresay that virtually everyone would tilt in the direction I tilted in, provided the quasi-pattern were sufficiently blatant. In any case, my personal threshold had been easily met, and so I started dismantling and rebuilding lines that only moments earlier I'd been most pleased with.

It was with surprising ease that I got twelve out of the fourteen lines to start with "T", and then another half hour or so turned the trick of the remaining two, and *voilà* — an Onegin stanza had just been born whose left edge obeyed a tight visual constraint and whose right edge obeyed a tight sonic constraint (not to mention the rhythmic constraint that pervaded each line, from left edge to right). At first, I had mixed feelings about this extra level of pattern that I'd added, feeling that it might reek of exhibitionism, but one stark fact convinced me that I should leave it in the new form: the anglicized stanza had, beyond any shadow of a doubt, been *improved* by the pattern-inspired modifications!

At this point, I'd done four out of about 400 stanzas, but still wasn't dreaming of tackling the whole book. To be sure, some people would see the beckoning pattern already at just 4/400, while for others, it might require having completed 350/400 before it would occur to them that they might as well go for broke... I, in any case, didn't yet see my destiny looming between the lines of what I'd done so far.

Another couple of months passed, and my mind was getting ever more loaded with new stanzas. At Christmas vacation, my mother, my sister's family, and my children and I all went to Hawaii for ten days, and there I was once again overcome by the beauty of certain stanzas — this time the trio with which Chapter VI concludes — and was once again invaded by the irresistible desire to "possess" them via translation. I did the first two of them while there, and when we returned to the mainland, I noticed a blank book that I had been given several months earlier, sitting untouched in some random pile of papers and books. Staring at it, I was all of a sudden hit by the thought: "That blank book has about 400 pages; *Eugene Onegin* has about 400 stanzas. Just think: one stanza on each page!"

The thought seemed quite ridiculous: me, with such sparse knowledge of Russian, hoping to clamber up this formidable Everest of translation, a book often said to be next to untranslatable, and square at the center of the inner circle of Russian literature! Yet it couldn't be denied that I'd *already* done six stanzas and, by George, they weren't all that bad! Who says you need to be a fluent speaker of Russian? My mind toyed with this idea. How long would it take? How much of my life would I have to devote to this preposterous endeavor? Could I afford the time? Why on earth would I want to do such a thing?

But the answer to the last question was simple: *love, sheer love.* And indeed, that answer was enough to override all other doubts, and in no time flat I was riffling the pages of that heretofore totally boring blank book and envisioning some future day when each one of those white sheets would be covered with black ink, with good lines, bad lines, crossings-out galore — and there was my future, beckoning me, staring me in the face, pulling me forward. My fate was sealed.

Lolling in Bed Sweet Bed with My Sultry Feminine Rhymes

From this crazy challenge there was clearly going to emerge one goal that I had dreamt of for decades — namely, I was going to learn a *lot* of Russian. Since I'd already done four stanzas of Chapter VII, I decided, quite arbitrarily, that that chapter was where I would begin, and in early January, I plunged in with ardor. It so happened that during the previous months my mood had been slipping gradually down a long slope, and by early January, I was in a state of great agitation and sadness. Life seemed nearly devoid of joy, and all felt bleak — all, that is, but my little stanzas. But now that I'd decided to tackle the whole book, things started looking up enormously. I found new strength and peace, even occasional exhilaration, when I was working on this task, and somehow *Eugene Onegin* pulled me right up out of one of my life's deepest pits.

Each morning, after getting my children up and off to school, I would return home and fix myself a cup of hazelnut coffee, pour some milk and a small boatload of sugar into it, carry it upstairs, and cozy up with the Russian text in bed — or as Carol used to call it, "bed sweet bed". At some point it crossed my mind that this cozy spot in which I was creating my own stanzas was exactly the spot where Carol and I had first read Johnston's and Falen's stanzas to each other with such delight, a realization that lent a double-edged poignancy to my toil.

Sipping my pseudo-coffee, I would start hunting for feminine rhymes to use in lines 1 and 3. It was always with a search for feminine rhymes that my work would have to start because, given how much more elusive they are than masculine rhymes, it's around their scaffolding that all else must be built. I'd think and think, pause for a little drink, think and think some more, now and then scribble down a list of potential rhymes or rough synonyms, and then, every so often, some exquisite feminine rhyme would come wafting into my mind from out of nowhere, solving a problem that had been plaguing me for a half hour or more, and for a few brief moments, I would know ecstasy.

Yes, strange to say, of all the pleasures I've known in life, those countless mornings spent lolling in bed sweet bed with my beautiful, elusive, sultry, seductive feminine rhymes, converting Pushkin's lilting Onegin stanzas into my own strange brand of poetry, rank close to the top. For various reasons of my own, I wound up doing first all the odd-numbered chapters in the order 7–1–3–5, and then tackled the even ones in the order 2–4–6–8. And day after day, I would flip the pages of my once-blank book and say to myself, "Twenty down, 358 to go!" Or else, "Finally I'm into three digits!" Or even better, "Fifty percent!" — a most memorable moment, which came on June 5.

My pace was very irregular. On lucky days, a good first draft of a full stanza would come within a mere hour, while on rough days, it could take three, possibly even four hours. But then the act of polishing, scattered in random episodes over the next few days or even weeks, added much more time. Nonetheless, there started to emerge a fairly clear pace: about 1.3 completed stanzas per day, on the average. To my delight, I could almost predict that sometime in the early fall of 1998, I would be done!

In order not to slow my pace at all, I made sure that every day, without exception, I worked on *Onegin*. Stanzas were thus done on vacations, on work-related trips, on countless airplane trips, in the car while I was driving one place or another, while I was sitting on the deck while the kids splashed away in friends' pools, while I was hiking with friends and family among remote lakes in the high Sierras, and on and on. Indeed, I'm always struck when I enumerate the widely-spread-out locales in which this translation was worked on: California, Hawaii, Indiana, Tennessee, Illinois, France, Switzerland, Italy, Bulgaria, Sweden... In my memory, each of these spots glows warmly with the special aura of the particular stanzas that I translated in it.

Pushkin's Last Stanza

But the most unexpected, the most glowing site of all was saved for the very last. In mid-summer 1998, I went to Sofia, Bulgaria, for a conference in cognitive science, and while there I found myself strangely drawn by the Slavic faces all around, and, reading signs in Bulgarian everywhere with surprising ease, I was tantalized by the sense of closeness to that other Slavic tongue with which I was now so intimately bound up. Almost inevitably, my thoughts jumped from Bulgaria to Russia, and a wild idea sprang unbidden into my head. I had a sabbatical year coming up very soon, in fact overlapping with Pushkin's bicentennial year — and so why not spend it in his own land, indeed in his own beloved city of Saint Petersburg?

Never had I set foot in Russia. The idea of spending a full year there, though deeply enticing, was also fraught with complexity, especially with respect to my children. For me, I envisioned a stint at the State University of Saint Petersburg, centered somehow on my involvement with Pushkin and translation, but for the kids? I couldn't just jump into such a situation blindly, and so once I was back in the United States, I set out planning an exploratory week-long jaunt to Petersburg, and the most natural date — in fact, the only workable date for me — was in mid-October. It did not escape me that with this timing, my trip would come close to coinciding with the date I foresaw for the completion of my *Onegin*, at which point the whole trip took on a certain eerie feeling of predestination.

Not long after I'd purchased my air ticket, the sudden terrible landslide of the ruble's value started, and what up till then had seemed an idyllic prospect for a sabbatical year started taking on ominous tones. I tried to keep an open mind, but making an exploratory visit seemed far more critical now. In any case, as my trip drew closer, I started counting days and stanzas very carefully, parceling out the latter in such a way as to ensure that I would have precisely three left to do when I arrived in Petersburg.

And then occurred a strange twist of fate. Ten months earlier, just before our Hawaiian vacation, at a gala fund-raiser in California to support a bicentennial Pushkin jubilee, I'd met a distant American relative of the Russian poet — Kenneth Pushkin, a man of most honest principles, an art dealer, a friendly fellow who was in fact dutifully respecting his name — pushing his kin, that is to say — by spearheading the bicentennial celebration in America. The two of us hit it off, and over the following months remained in contact. I knew Kenneth did much business in Russia, so in early September, a month or so before taking off, I tried phoning him at home in Albuquerque in order to get some hints about hotels and contact people in Petersburg, only to find out that just that day he himself had taken off for Petersburg for a month, and I got his phone number there. This was a stroke of luck for me, partly because during the next few weeks I was able to call Kenneth up frequently to get a first-hand sense of all the turmoil I was reading about in the papers. But Kenneth also happened to be placed in the most strategic imaginable way to help me in my visit: he was in daily contact with key people at the

All-Russia Pushkin Museum, and thus through him, in the twinkling of an eye, I had a link to people as involved as anyone in Russia in preserving Pushkin's legacy.

Given this fortuitous link, I couldn't resist the temptation to ask whether, during my brief October visit, I might not be able to give a small reading somewhere of selections from my translation. Within a day or two, the answer came back from the Museum's director, Sergei Nekrasov: he proposed I give one in a series of readings called "Poets from Around the World", as part of a traditional October literary festival in the idyllic rural town now called Pushkin, formerly called Tsarskoe Selo — "the czar's village" — where Pushkin had gone to a special, elite boarding school in his adolescence. I was very gratified by this unusually warm reception, and of course accepted without delay.

Egged on by success, I upped my level of chutzpah one more notch, and inquired whether, a day or two before my reading, I might be granted the privilege of translating the very last stanza of *Eugene Onegin* in Pushkin's apartment along the Moika Canal in Petersburg. This time, the response took a little longer in coming back, but to my great joy, it too was positive: the day before my Tsarskoe Selo reading, I would be given a couple of hours to "commune with Pushkin" alone in his apartment, and to do the final stanza. Since for me, this had always been one of the most affecting of all the stanzas in the book, and since in it, the poet bids a final farewell to his novel and his beloved Tanya and Eugene, it seemed the perfect way for me, too, to bid farewell to my translation and to all the multiple meanings with which it of late had so graced my life.

And thus, at 5:00 in the evening of Friday, October 16, 1998, I found myself being ushered into the elegant book-lined drawing room of Alexander Pushkin's hallowed apartment — in fact, into the very *stanza* in which Pushkin died from wounds received in his duel — and there I was left in solitude, so that I could calmly spread out all my working materials on a dark wooden table and make myself comfortable on a couch just below a large portrait of the poet. Aside from a clock somewhere, I was immersed in total silence, and the last stanza's familiar words looked up at me from the novel's last page.

It was hard to believe that only a year and a half earlier, I hadn't read a single stanza of *Eugene Onegin* in Russian, while now I knew nearly fifty of them by heart and had translated nearly 400 of them into English, and now here I was, alone in Saint Petersburg with Pushkin's spirit — or at least with his portrait — just about to tackle the novel's very last fourteen-line crystal. And I'd been allotted precisely two hours to carry out this crowning task, and there was that clock, ticking softly away. Time to stop musing and set to work.

As was the case with every stanza, my opponent's opening gambit was the first pair of feminine rhymes — lines 1 and 3. What was my move? In my usual way, I thought and thought about the first quatrain and how it could be reworded in rhyming English, but nothing came, and tick tick tick, the game clock kept ticking away. I read and reread the Russian lines, even though I could say them in my sleep. Nothing I thought of worked.

A half hour passed, then forty minutes; still I hadn't written one word. I was starting to feel pretty antsy. What if, given this once-in-a-lifetime chance, I blew it? This fear compounded my nervousness, of course, starting what could be a vicious circle. But all at once, perhaps forty-five minutes into my allotted time, a little idea flashed into mind that felt *right*. How well I knew that tremor of excitement at a potential solution to a difficult pair of lines! I scribbled it down, and suddenly the logjam was broken. The first quatrain was coming into focus; things were feeling looser, more fluid. I had a hunch I was going to win this game.

"My uncle …… mine."

For months and months, long before I'd dreamt of making a pilgrimage to Saint Petersburg, I'd anticipated the moment of finishing up my very own *Onegin*, knowing it would inevitably be a time of great emotional complexity: an intimate mixture of relief, joy, and pride, on the one hand, with, on the other, deep sadness at the fact of closing the book on this bizarre, beloved adventure. Though I'd had no idea as to how it would feel in detail, there was nonetheless one tiny fact about the final moment of translation that my magic crystal had been telling me for months, with every bit as much certainty as an astronomer will tell you where and when an eclipse will occur, and that was what the word would be with which my work would wind up — to wit, the word "mine".

The reason underlying this peculiar predictability was just as compelling as it was simple: Pushkin's novel's first stanza's first word is мой ("my"), while its last stanza's last word is моим (a variant of the same word — namely, the instrumental case of мой). That was quite enough for me. It was not that I knew that Pushkin had intended this little symmetry; indeed, it could well be a mere coincidence, and it's doubtful whether anyone will ever know the truth of the matter. But intentional or not, this echoing of the takeoff in the act of landing was an elegant structural property of the original Russian, and once having noticed it, I couldn't imagine failing to mirror it in my English rendering.

Though the minutes were ticking away quickly now, my lines too were clicking like clockwork. Before I knew it, there I was, zeroing in on that final line, that inevitable final masculine "mine" — and then, truly as though gifts straight from heaven, first one, then two, then three masculine lines, each of them rhyming with the preordained final one, came tumbling into my fervid brain. Everything fell smoothly into place, and ten minutes before I was to turn into a pumpkin, my stanza, my chapter, and my translation as a whole were done.

In those remaining ten minutes, savoring the fact of having scaled this metaphorical Everest, I took in the scenery around me for the first time, wandering gingerly about Pushkin's last *stanza*, actually noticing the portrait under which I had been sitting, seeing the sheet music on the clavichord, trying to decipher words from the manuscript of a poem in a notebook that had been sitting right by my notebook as I toiled away. Then, having snapped a few photographs, I hunted around for the apartment's caretaker, thanked her, and stepped out into the brisk evening air. Moments later, Greg ambled into view along the Moika Canal, and in a festive mood, the two of us sauntered off to celebrate, over dinner, the reaching of this long-awaited goal.

Walter Arndt's Symmetric Translation

It turns out I'm not the only translator who noticed and opted to respect the novel's *мой–моим* symmetry; there was one other — the prolific and versatile Walter Arndt. He, too, imitated the gesture, though in a cleverly different manner. Arndt's first line runs, "Now that he is in grave condition", while his closing line is: "As I to my Onegin now." Once again, I'm not sure the symmetry is deliberate, but given Arndt's astuteness, I would bet it is.

Stylistically, Arndt's *Onegin* differs vastly from mine. If I err on the side of too much modernity and informality, I would say that Arndt errs on the side of too much classicism and formality. The tone of Pushkin's language falls somewhere in between these poles. Despite this often troubling tendency, Arndt's version has many virtues, and quite a few marvelous stanzas. Here, for example, is stanza IV.20 in Arndt's delightful rendition:

> *Heigh ho… Sweet reader, let me question,*
> *How is your family? All well?*
> *If you don't mind the mere suggestion*
> *And are at leisure, let me tell*
> *The proper meaning of "relations".*
> *Here goes, then, word and connotations:*
> *Folk to be earnestly revered,*
> *Deferred to, cosseted, and cheered;*
> *At Christmas, thus decrees convention,*
> *One goes to see them without fail*
> *Or sends them greetings through the mail,*
> *Just to be paid no more attention*
> *For the remainder of the year…*
> *A ripe old age God grant them here!*

Arndt's anglicization of *Eugene Onegin* came out in 1963 and was generally well received; indeed, it was honored by that year's Bollingen Prize for poetry translation.

Nabokov Hopes for Yet Greater Ugliness

The following year, the famed Russian–American writer Vladimir Nabokov published an extensive scholarly commentary on *Eugene Onegin*, which was accompanied by what he termed a "pony" — a line-by-line literal translation of the novel-in-verse, making no attempt at rhyme, rhythm, or literary grace. Now, the idea of a line-by-line gloss of *Eugene Onegin* is certainly not in itself a bad one. Such a work could be used in many ways: by other translators, by students of the Russian language and its literature, by literary scholars with a medium command of Russian, and so forth. However, Nabokov was not content to offer his version as one among many possible approaches; harshly denouncing all rivals, he shrilly proclaimed his own vision as the only "true" vision. Thus in the foreword to his literal translation, he wrote:

> ...it is when the translator sets out to render the "spirit", and not the mere sense of the text, that he begins to traduce his author.
>
> In transposing *Eugene Onegin* from Pushkin's Russian into my English I have sacrificed to completeness of meaning every formal element including the iambic rhythm, whenever its retention hindered fidelity. To my ideal of literalism I sacrificed everything (elegance, euphony, clarity, good taste, modern usage, and even grammar) that the dainty mimic prizes higher than truth.

Nabokov's scorn for the *dainty mimic* who would eschew *truth* in favor of "spirit" (here I quote his quote-marks, of course) of the original is puzzling, to say the least. It amounts to taking a fanatical attitude toward originals and translations — namely, that a work can be appreciated only in its original language, and that no attempt should be made to reproduce the *feel* of the work in any other language. Those poor saps who are ignorant of the original tongue are simply doomed to remain deprived of that experience, and the closest they can come to imagining what it must be like for lucky natives is by reading an always awkward, often opaque word-for-word gloss, while thinking to themselves, "Oh, but in Russian this comes out as sparkling, lilting, delicious poetry that one absorbs without any effort whatsoever."

Reading Nabokov's gawky "pony" and his commentary is a bit like taking a long mountain hike in a severe blizzard, chilled to the bone, dead tired, able to see but a few inches beyond one's nose, while being subjected to a ceaseless barrage of remarks from one's companion, who yammers on and on about how it feels to come skipping merrily along the same trail on a sunny day amidst brilliant fields of spring blossoms, with all the names of said blossoms (as well as trees) provided in Latin, not to mention the names of nearby peaks, plus a deep well of sagas of local loggers, loiterers, and litterers, a detailed history of the Wilderness Act, and so on and so forth ... One would get far more from staying at home and just watching a video of the springtime hike than from making the "true" hike in this eccentrically sadistic manner.

Let's take a look, for instance, at how Nabokov, in his "pony", renders the stanza we saw above as done by Arndt:

> *Hm, hm, gent reader,*
> *is your entire kin well?*
> *Allow me; you might want, perhaps,*
> *to learn now from me*
> *what "kinsfolks" means exactly?*
> *Well, here's what kinsfolks are:*
> *we are required to pet them,*
> *love them, esteem them cordially,*
> *and, following popular custom,*
> *come Christmas, visit them,*
> *or else congratulate them postally,*
> *so that for the rest of the year*
> *they will not think about us.*
> *So grant them, God, long life!*

The British critic and *Onegin* co-translator A. D. P. Briggs has written incisively of the cult of "Pushkinolatry", whose adherents bow deeply before Pushkin's works, as if every thought, every metaphor — indeed, every word — must have come from the gods. Vladimir Nabokov is, no doubt, the high priest of this cult.

Although in his younger years he translated verse into verse with great gusto (including Pushkin), he declares in the foreword to his crib that the task of translating *Onegin* while respecting both form and content is "mathematically impossible" (as if less heroic acts of form-plus-content translation had somehow been proven "mathematically possible", but literature-loving mathematicians had demonstrated with ironclad rigor that *Onegin* falls in a totally different category). If one takes Nabokov's peculiar declarations at face value, one must conclude that he believes that to read a hideously ugly literal translation is the sole path to Pushkinian truth for a non-speaker of Russian, and that to produce such a version is the only way for a translator to show adequate respect for Pushkin's holy opus. To translate Pushkin's verse *as verse* is to desecrate the novel, is to spit on the tomb of its author.

A couple of years after his commentary and crib were published, Nabokov made the following remarks about his prosaic offering in a belligerent article called "Reply to My Critics":

> My *Eugene Onegin* falls short of the ideal crib. It is still not close enough and not ugly enough. In future editions I plan to defowlerize it still more drastically. I think I shall turn it entirely into utilitarian prose, with a still bumpier brand of English, rebarbative barricades of square brackets and tattered banners of reprobate words, in order to eliminate the last vestiges of bourgeois poesy and concession to rhythm. This is something to look forward to.

And thus was rendered inevitable a brutal collision between Nabokov and Arndt, wearing their hats as translators of the same work of literature, a work equally revered by both, but in very different ways.

The Sacred Quiddity and Eyespot of a Poet's Genius

To give just the smallest sample of how Nabokov did his best to decimate his rival in print, I'll quote a tiny piece of a huge, sprawling attack on Arndt's translation, which Nabokov first published in *The New York Review of Books* in 1964, and later reprinted in his book *Strong Opinions*. The topic is the first few lines of stanza VI.36 (Друзья мои, вам жаль поэта: / Во цвете радостных надежд, / Их не свершив ещё для света, / Чуть из младенческих одежд, / Увял!) which I would render literally this way: "My friends, the poet grieves you: / In the bloom of joyful hopes, / But not yet having realized them for the world, / Barely out of infant clothing, / He withered!", and which Arndt rhymingly and rhythmically renders as follows: "My friends, you will lament the poet / Who, flowering with a happy gift, / Must wilt before he could bestow it / Upon the world, yet scarce adrift / From boyhood's shore." Here is how Nabokov comments upon these lines, in Arndt's rendering:

Passive readers will derive, no doubt, a casual illusion of sense from Arndt's actually nonsensical line 2 of VI.36. They will hardly notice that the chancrous metaphor in lines 4–5 inflicted by a meretricious rhyme is not Pushkin's fault, nor wonder at the naïve temerity a paraphrast has of throwing in his own tropes when he should know that the figure of speech is the main, sacred quiddity and eyespot of a poet's genius, and is the last thing that should be tampered with.

A certain haughtiness comes through here, does it not? One might suppose that Nabokov's own rendering of these lines would be a breath of fresh air, but no such luck: "My friends, you're sorry for the poet: / in the bloom of glad hopes, / not having yet fulfilled them for the world, / scarce out of infant clothes, / has withered!" It's hardly enticing prose, let alone lyrical poetry, and on top of that, it is quite in vain that one searches for the subject of the verb "has withered".

These samples we've had of Nabokov's idiosyncratic rendering of *Eugene Onegin* are typical, though they are far from the most awkward of passages. And yet, of all anglicizations of Pushkin's novel-in-verse, Nabokov's is by far the best known and, in my experience, the most frequently found on bookstore shelves. Why would this be? Because the name of the author of *Lolita* is far better known than those of James Falen, Charles Johnston, Walter Arndt, Oliver Elton, A. D. P. Briggs, or Babette Deutsch. And why are these names little known? To some extent, it's because they are translators, and in our culture, translators — even the best literary translators — are seen largely as drones. But also, to a fair degree, they are little known because the author of *Lolita* mercilessly trashed their translations (Falen's and Johnston's he never saw, thanks to mortality, but since he trashed verse–verse translation *in general,* he effectively trashed all future versions as well as all past ones), and because a star-struck and gullible public bought the glittery Nabokovian pontification on credit.

Scholars of Russian literature, of course, know better, and they generally look upon Nabokov's bitter, relentless attacks on verse translators of *Onegin* as the rantings of an eccentric genius, and let it go at that. The tragedy, though, is that upon literature-loving non-readers of Russian, the Nabokovian dogma has been foisted, and by them has by and large been swallowed whole. All over the English-speaking world, highly placed literary scholars who know no Russian seem to think Nabokov's repellent, wooden crib is *the* translation, and that all flowing, metrical, rhyming translations of *Onegin* are necessarily works of misguided amateurish buffoonery. As a consequence, most have probably never looked at any of the verse translations, and hence never tasted the exquisite beauty of Pushkin's novel. Such, sadly, can be the influence wielded by a ceaselessly self-promoting silver-tongue with a famous name.

Deutsch, Johnston, and Elton/Briggs

When I wrote my comparative review of *Onegin* versifications for *The New York Times* as well as my more extensive chapters on the same topic in *Le Ton beau de Marot*, I knew there was one verse translation into English that I had not seen. That one, from the pen of Babette Deutsch, had been published in 1936 and was out of print. The library's copy was checked out, and despite various attempts to recall it, I was unable to lay my hands on it. But one day, soon after my review appeared in the *Times*, I received in the mail an unexpected present from Kelly Holt, a professor of Theater Arts at Case Western Reserve University, whom I had once met in the apartment of Lil Greenberg, an elderly mutual friend in Cleveland. Lil had in the meantime died and given many books away to friends, among which was the very translation that I lacked, in a handsome clothbound edition with a slipcover. Having read my piece in the *Times*, Kelly felt that I, as an *Onegin* savorer, could probably put the Deutsch translation to better use than she could, so she sent it to me and I accepted it gratefully, thinking of it in a way as a posthumous gift from Lil.

I dipped into it and before long, I realized that this translation appealed to me more than did any other except Falen's. Here, to give you a sense of Deutsch's deft touch, is the same stanza as we've already seen from the pens of Arndt and Nabokov:

> *H'm, h'm! Dear reader, pray apprise me,*
> *Are all your relatives quite well?*
> *You might be pleased — if so, advise me —*
> *To have your humble servant tell*
> *What the word "relatives" embraces.*
> *It means the people to whose faces*
> *We show at all times due respect,*
> *And whom we kiss as they expect,*
> *And visit at the Christmas season,*
> *Unless indeed we send a card*
> *In token of our warm regard,*
> *Lest they should miss us beyond reason*
> *All during the ensuing year.*
> *And so God grant them health and cheer!*

Deutsch's *Eugene Onegin* has the virtues of simplicity and clarity, as one sees here, and usually of rhythmic smoothness as well.

I now present two further versions of the same stanza, the first of them taken from Sir Charles Johnston's 1977 translation — the one that so inspired Vikram Seth:

> *Hm, hm. Distinguished reader, tell me*
> *how are your <u>kith and kin</u> today?*
> *And here my sentiments impel me*
> *for your enlightenment to say*
> *how I interpret this expression:*
> *our kin are folk whom by profession*
> *we have to cherish and admire*
> *with all our hearts, and who require*
> *that in the usual Christmas scrimmage*
> *we visit them, or without fail*
> *send them good wishes through the mail*
> *to ensure that till next time our image*
> *won't even cross their minds by stealth...*
> *God grant them years and years of health!*

Although this stanza flows fairly well (except for line 12, which has ten instead of nine syllables — a flaw that can be righted if one pronounces "to ensure" as "twinsure"), it just doesn't have the directness and charm of Deutsch's stanza.

Far more problematical, unfortunately, is Oliver Elton's translation, published in 1937, the centennial of Pushkin's death:

> *Ahem! Most honoured reader, let me*
> *Ask, — are your family all well?*
> *And might it please you to permit me*
> *This opportunity to tell*
> *The accurate signification*
> *Of the words "family", "relation"?*
> *— With love and kindness we are bound*
> *To treat relations; with profound*
> *Respectfulness; to go to see them*
> *At Yule — our custom national;*
> *Or, through the post, to greet them all.*
> *Thus, for the twelvemonth, you will free them*
> *From giving you one thought; and so,*
> *Long years God grant them, here below!*

There are several annoying glitches in this stanza, and as one reads more and more of Elton's version — even as modified a few decades later by A. D. P. Briggs — one finds that it often falls short of Pushkinian standards along one dimension or another.

Finally, a Pushkin Translation Truly à la Pushkin

The legendary harpichordist Wanda Landowska once proudly remarked to another musician, "You play Bach your way; I play him *his* way." There is a certain charmingly Nabokovian hubris to her comment, and it's easy for me to imagine Nabokov saying to a rival translator, "You render Pushkin in your style; I render him in *his* style." But of course such a claim would be patent nonsense, Pushkin's Russian style being anything but "bourgeois", "bumpy", "rebarbative", or bulging to the brim with "reprobate words".

On the other hand, if ever anyone were entitled to make such a remark, it would be James Falen. I hasten to add that it would be outrageously out of character for Falen to trumpet himself in that way, but I feel I can take the liberty of doing it for him. It was, after all, through Falen's version that Carol and I first were enchanted by Pushkin's style, and it was through a deeper involvement with his translation that I subsequently fell head over heels in love with *Onegin*. Since then, I've shown Falen's *Onegin* to many Russians, and it evokes a near-universal reaction of astonishment along these lines: "I've looked at other attempts in English and always been disappointed; never would I have believed that Pushkin's deeply Russian flavor could be captured in any other language — but this, well, it sounds *just like* Pushkin."

And I myself, having now read the original *Onegin* at least 100 times and Falen's *Onegin* at least two dozen times, feel Falen has come as close to writing what Pushkin himself would have written, had he been an English speaker, as is humanly possible to imagine. Let's just take a look at this same old stanza IV.20, which gets Falen's style across pretty well, although, to tell the truth, it is a rather run-of-the-mill effort for him:

> *Hm, hm, dear reader, feeling mellow?*
> *And are your kinfolk well today?*
> *Perhaps you'd like, you gentle fellow,*
> *To hear what I'm prepared to say*
> *On "kinfolk" and their implications?*
> *Well, here's my view of close relations:*
> *They're people whom we're bound to prize,*
> *To honor, love, and idolize,*
> *And, following the old tradition,*
> *To visit come the Christmas feast,*
> *Or send a wish by mail at least;*
> *All other days they've our permission*
> *To quite forget us, if they please —*
> *So grant them, God, long life and ease!*

It reads effortlessly, both semantically and rhythmically, and no wonder, since, like the original Russian, it is 100 percent iambic. Indeed, Falen made a much more concerted effort than all of his predecessors to write in iambs, though on rare occasions he will resort to a trochee or two in a stanza (strong–weak, instead of weak–strong). He also strove to make his sentences flow as naturally as speech, since that's how Pushkin's sentences flow. And his vocabulary floats midway between the modern and the antique — a kind of timeless, placeless English, hinting vaguely of the past. But Falen also excels on less tangible levels, such as narrator's tone, use of irony, reluctance to resort to rare words, sense of wit and snap, degree of inter-stanza homogeneity, use of sonic repetition, and on and on.

Why Try It Yourself If You Feel It's Been Done Perfectly?

At this point, I hear my readers aching to ask me, "Why on earth would you want to do your own translation, if you so admire Falen's?" Well, I would ask them back: Did people stop climbing Everest when Hillary and Tenzing had climbed it? Does a good pianist stop playing a work simply because great recordings of it already exist? Of course not. People are driven to do their own thing precisely because of the wonderful accomplishments of others. In my case, it was Falen's magical artistry that first of all made me want to experience the original, and secondly made me want to do something similar, yet different, in my native tongue.

If anything, Falen's translation *liberated* me to do a translation in my own style. What I mean by this is that, had he not done such an extraordinary job in his translation, I would have felt far more constrained to restrain myself at each decision point (of which there are a myriad myriad, needless to say), to be "more

Pushkinlike" than my natural tuning would wish. But since Falen had already done a translation *parfaitement à la Pouchkine*, I could instead go off and do my own thing, and feel not the slightest trace of guilt about it.

Thus here is an example — once again, stanza IV.20 — in the Hofstadter style:

> *Hallo, hulloo, my gentle reader!*
> *And how're your kinfolk, old and young?*
> *Pray let me tell you, as your leader,*
> *Some scuttlebutt about our tongue.*
> *What's "kin"? It's relatively subtle,*
> *But you'll tune in if I but scuttle:*
> *Our kith and kin we're meant to love;*
> *We dish out kisses, tokens of*
> *Our high esteem; we pay a visit*
> *Each Christmas — it's a Russian rut —*
> *Or else send notes in greeting, but...*
> *It isn't out of fondness, is it?*
> *It's all so they'll forget forthwith*
> *Us kin — and so let's toast our kith!*

I do not find it all that easy to articulate the characteristics of my style, but since the greatest influence on me was James Falen himself (though Vikram Seth, too, had deep impact), I tend to contrast my style with his, and so I sometimes say that where Falen is lyrical, I am jazzy, or where he's legato, I'm staccato, or where he's flowing, I'm percussive, or where he's subtly seasoned, I'm saucy and spicy.

In any case, one of my traits, here very easy to see, is a love for playing with repeated sounds, as in "scuttlebutt", "subtle, but", and "but scuttle". A closely related trait is a proneness to indulge in alliteration: "Russian rut" provides a simple example, as do the phrases "fondness" and "forget forthwith" near the end. I'm also fond of internal rhymes, as exemplified by "What's kin" and "tune in" on successive lines. Yet another tendency of mine is to play on slightly buried resonances of a word or phrase, such as using the adverb "relatively" in a stanza whose topic is kinfolk.

A friend of mine, after reading first Falen's *Onegin* and then mine, commented that he hadn't realized, until reading my version, how unconventional and startling Pushkin's language must have seemed to readers in his day; Falen's version didn't convey that quality of Pushkin at all clearly. I had to smile when I heard this, because such an impression is quite wrong; it is Falen who gives a truly accurate reflection of Pushkin's tone, not I — though how could my friend have known that?

I'm not into self-flagellation, and I'm certainly not espousing here the Nabokovian line that my translation's tone constitutes a shameful betrayal of Pushkin; I'm just objectively observing that my tone is a tad less similar to Pushkin's than Falen's is. But my "sinning" in this regard is not unique; the fact is that *all* the translators prior to Falen deviate from Pushkin's tone in quite substantive ways. Indeed, that's precisely why Russian readers are so astonished when they encounter Falen's work. And so, dear reader of my preface, I suggest that if you don't read Russian and if you find, either before or after reading the present translation, that you have a hankering to experience even more directly those beautiful vernal mountain meadows of the Russian original, you go out and get yourself a copy of Falen. You'll never come closer to tasting the true taste of Pushkin than that.

But that in itself doesn't invalidate my effort. One doesn't always stick to one's favorite dish when dining at a favorite restaurant; sometimes one selects another one, for variety's sake. Variety is the spice of life! And I, in my own way, bring out certain rather subtle spices in the lovely brew that is Pushkin's style by turning up various knobs a bit.

Thus, for instance, Pushkin and I share a keen enjoyment of alliteration, but I indulge in it to a greater degree than he does, on the average. This can be seen as a defect or as a virtue of my version. If Falen's translation didn't exist, my turning up of the alliteration knob would probably be less justifiable — but it *does* exist; someone's already done it at just the right level. Why should I try to repeat what Falen did? I would doubtless do less well at the task — and in any case I feel, somewhat paradoxically, that I have been liberated by Falen's translation, liberated and encouraged to explore territory that I am more cut out for. It's my hope that, precisely because of my natural tendencies to push a little extra in certain stylistic directions, my translation will find a friendly audience in the contemporary English-speaking world, a world that, after all, tends to go for things that are somewhat bigger than life.

In *Le Ton beau de Marot*, I self-deprecatingly wrote that I am a selfish translator, and that the only reason I do translation is to come in ever closer touch with the original author, purely for my own pleasure. But I take that back here. When I compare myself with Vladimir Nabokov, I see that I am, in fact, a generous translator. I deeply desire to share with others the thrill of being in close touch with Pushkin, a thrill that I first experienced through James Falen's English version of *Eugene Onegin*, and, some years later, through Alexander Pushkin's Russian version. I want now to make that experience more widely available to anglophones, whether through my own translation, through Falen's, through Deutsch's, through Arndt's, or whatever.

"I Will Now Proceed to Decode…

Throughout his lifetime fascinated by foreign languages and by complex acts of translation, the American statistician and pioneering computer scientist Warren Weaver was among the first to propose the idea of machine translation, and in a famous paper that he once wrote on the topic, he declared, "When I look at an article in Russian, I say, *This is really written in English, but it has been coded in some strange symbols. I will now proceed to decode.*" This has to be one of the funniest things I've ever heard said about translation — and yet I know exactly how Weaver could feel that way. Indeed, each morning, when I plunked myself down in bed with my coffee by my side, I'd don my trusty Warren Weaver cap and duly *proceed to decode.*

I'd like to make one thing very clear, at this point: Though far from a fluent speaker of the Russian tongue, I always worked *from the Russian* and from the Russian *alone* (either memorized or on paper in front of me). In fact, I studiously avoided looking at other anglicizations, even though, of course, I'd read bits and pieces of them all, and in Falen's case, had read the whole thing cover to cover several times. Fearful at first of having been unwittingly contaminated by the excellent work of others, I soon discovered, to my relief, when I compared my stanzas with those of my "rivals", that nothing of their texts jumped into my mind claiming falsely to be of my own invention; no, my rhymes and ways of phrasing things were almost always quite different from anyone else's. Whew!

Of course there were occasions when I found I'd come up with just the same pair of rhymes as someone else did, but that was pretty rare. Worst of all was that handful of times when I came up with a solution that I loved and that I thought was so very much *me,* only to find that Babette Deutsch or Oliver Elton, way back in the 1930's, had turned over exactly the same stone. Frustrating! But truth to tell, I found that for the most part, my own version overlapped less with preceding ones than they overlapped with each other. And thus it was clear that I was not a plagiarist, either wittingly or unwittingly.

...with a Little Help from My Friends"

I said above that I never looked at any English input text, but I have to retract that. Once in a blue moon, being but a baby speaker of Russian, I would in fact find myself having to resort to napping briefly in Nabokov's crib. This was necessitated when, after staring and staring and struggling and struggling, I simply could not for the life of me figure out what the Russian meant — my well-worn Kenneth Katzner dictionary, much though I loved it, just was not sufficient to pull me out of the pit. This happened probably a few times per chapter at the outset, and gradually less as time went on. On such humiliating occasions, I would glance only at the specific lines in question and then quickly shut the book before my eyes could take in any more of the rebarbative and reprobate, bourgeois and bumpy Nabokovian turns of phrase. Obviously, I felt a little weird about using my nemesis as my consultant, but it seemed slightly less shameful when I found out that I was in good company — even Johnston and Arndt and Falen had ridden the VN pony once in a while themselves.

The greatest joy was afforded me each time I completed the first draft of a new stanza, for it was then that I allowed myself to open up all five of my "rivals" in order to see what solutions they'd found to exactly the problems that I'd just been tangling with. I always began with Falen and always finished up with Deutsch, in order to maximize pleasure at beginning and end, and each time I would read Falen's, I would sigh and say to myself, "Ahh... Now *that's* how you translate poetry!" Still and all, I generally felt I more or less held my own with the others, even if I couldn't reach Falen's level of artistry. It was the friendliest of competitions, and I felt I was getting to know each translator quite well.

Making these comparisons was not just fun but also served, as it turned out, a very useful purpose — namely, as a way of making sure I did not put my foot in my mouth. Yes, though I hate to admit it, there were a few occasions on which I made a total fool of myself, thinking I'd perfectly understood a passage and then discovering that all the other translators had read it in a different manner. Sometimes it was just that I'd been confused about a noun's or adjective's declension; other times it was subtler. In any case, though, my "rivals" showed their true colors by helping me out, just like good friends.

In a couple of cases, I found my very own interpretation for certain lines, breaking decisively with the prevailing winds. The most noteworthy of these cases was the famous suite of five stanzas in Chapter I to which Nabokov gave the rebarbative label "pedal digression". It is in these stanzas that Pushkin seems to reveal that he is a foot fetishist — but I say "seems" advisedly. To be precise, the word Pushkin uses — нога — is a notorious Russian word that means both "foot" and "leg" (and my Russian friends assure me that its diminutive form, ножка, which Pushkin also uses in the "pedal digression", is no less ambiguous) — and therefore, in his sensual pæan to sleek pairs of feminine appendages, Pushkin is referring just as plausibly to *legs* as to *feet*. Indeed, every single Russian whom I have consulted — mostly females, I might add — has been absolutely convinced that "leg" and not "foot" is what Pushkin had in mind. I've thus bucked the heretofore universal and slightly puritanical trend to say "feet", and in my version of the pedal digression, which Greg Huber has amusingly called my "iambic diversion", I present Pushkin as a "leg man" rather than a foot fetishist. In rendering нога and ножка in English, I have used not just one word over and over, but rather, a whole spectrum of words that run admiringly up and down milady's limb, all the way from top… to bottom.

Poetic Lie-sense

An enthusiastic non-Russian-speaking friend to whom I once read out loud my version of Tatyana's letter exclaimed, "Doug, how did you ever learn all the subtle nuances of those Russian words?" What she imagined, at least so it seemed, was that I was taking each Russian word and somehow finding its perfect English counterpart, thus building up a sequence of perfect counterparts, and then, lo and behold, what came out was a flawlessly rhyming, flawless iambic-tetrameter poem! Regrettably, such a scenario is "mathematically impossible", as some authority once memorably phrased it.

The truth of the matter is that the name of the game is — and here Nabokov hits the nail right on the head — *paraphrasing*. Of course, Nabokov's pet word for someone who indulges in this shameful act — "paraphrast" — fairly reeks of contempt, but Nabokov notwithstanding, paraphrasing is the only way to go, in poetry translation. But given the negative aura around this term, thanks to Nabokov's constant nagging, I would propose an alternate name for the art of compromise in poetry translation — I would say that poetry translation is the art of "poetic lie-sense".

Yes, one is always lying, for to translate is to lie. But even to speak is to lie, no less. No word is perfect, no sentence captures all the truth and only the truth. All we do is make do, and in poetry, hopefully do so gracefully.

I do not, I freely though ruefully admit, have a mastery of all those subtle nuances of the Russian words I was translating. I have, rather, a *basic* sense of what each one means — I know the ballpark it's in. Thus благородный, for example, which occurs in a few of the stanzas that I've memorized, means to me "noble", and I can also see inside it to its roots, which tell me that it originally meant "well-born" (and as ever-observant Greg pointed out to me, so does the name "Eugene"). But I don't feel, when I hear it, the rich resonances that a native speaker of Russian must feel; I just think to myself, "noble", and then let any synonym or even roughly related word spring to mind. "Aristocratic"? Fine. "High-born"? Fine. "Fine"? Perhaps. And so forth.

What matters is not getting each and every word to match perfectly in connotations, but getting the overall *sense* and the overall *tone* of a line across, and doing so with an elegant rhythm and a high-quality rhyme, to boot. That's what matters. Rhythm, rhyme, sense, and tone — all of them together are what *Eugene Onegin* is about, and not just literal meaning. To throw any of these overboard is to destroy the poem utterly.

I have exploited poetic lie-sense so many times in making this translation that it's almost silly to try to pick examples — just take any line whatsoever! For instance, line 1 of stanza I.1. In the original, it runs as follows: Мой дядя самых честных правил, which could be literally rendered as "My uncle, of most honest principles", and phonetically rendered as *Moj dyádya sámykh chéstnykh právil.* But my translation's opening line runs this way: "My uncle, matchless moral model". As you see, already in line 1 of stanza I.1 I have introduced alliteration where there is none, I have used concepts like "morality" and "role model" that are not spelled out explicitly in the original, and with my choice of the word "matchless" I have perhaps wound up somewhat overstating the uniqueness of the speaker's uncle's admirable character traits. Compromise lies everywhere.

Let's skip lines 2 and 3, which also lie, though perhaps slightly less egregiously, and let's go on to line 4 — И лучше выдумать не мог, in Russian — "And couldn't have dreamt up [anything] better", *I lúchshe výdumat' ne mog,* literally and phonetically. But what yours truly writes on line 4 is, "Of all his ploys, that takes the cake", thus using a fairly jazzy idiomatic expression that probably most non-native readers wouldn't even know. What can I say about such brazen lying, and so early on, to boot? That really takes the cake.

Let's jump to the concluding line of the opening stanza: Когда же чёрт возьмёт тебя? (*Kogdá zhe chyort voz'myót tebyá?* — "When *will* the Devil take you, then?") Here, through my placement of the words "hurry" and "up", I indulge in a small piece of wordplay: "Hurry, dear Uncle, up and die!" To non-native readers, this almost surely parses as if it said, "Hurry up, dear Uncle — and die!", while to most American readers, it probably comes across with a more down-home flavor: "Hurry, dear Uncle — up-and-die!" There is nothing remotely like that

Translator's Preface

droll ambiguity in Pushkin's line, unless someone argued that its sharp bite, due especially to the words же чёрт, is somehow "equivalent" to my line's playfulness.

For one last example, let's look at the concluding line of the novel's second stanza: Но вреден север для меня (*No vréden séver dlya menyá* — "But harmful is the North to me"). Here, Pushkin is subtly (or not so subtly) alluding to the fact that it was from the northern town of Petersburg that he was sent by the czar into exile in southern Russia, for nothing more serious than having written a few slightly irreverent poems. Falen says here, "But found it noxious in the north", thus using poetic lie-sense by introducing alliteration where there was none, and also — if you want to be nitpicky — by having the chutzpah to change present into past. Arndt says, "The North, though, disagrees with me." Johnston: "but I'm allergic to the North…" Elton/Briggs: "But baneful is the North to me…" And finally, here is Deutsch: "But find the North is not my style."

By contrast, my translation says: "The North was, shall I say, 'severe'." By golly, I don't just toy around with tenses; I also sin in a big-time way by playing on the fact that the Russian word for "north" is pronounced *séver*. To some readers, this flippancy of mine will come across as so irreverent towards Pushkin that they would exile *me* to Bessarabia if they had the chance; to others, it will merely seem amusing. As for me, I see it as just another typical example of poetic lie-sense, and a quite Pushkinesque one, if I don't say so myself.

My translation abounds in this kind of thing, and if you don't like it, just set it down. Remember, there's always Falen, Deutsch, Arndt, and the others. Or else — why not? — you can just go and translate the whole thing yourself! It'll be a great opportunity for you to brush up on your Russian, that's for sure.

Personal Musings on Fluid Syllable-lengths, Dubious Rhymes, and Biased Perspectives

Here I'll take just a few paragraphs to describe some of my guiding principles in doing this translation, and to explain a little the rationale behind some stylistic choices.

One of the most central maxims that I've tried to abide by is that of *covering my tracks* as far as rhymes are concerned. By this, I mean that a reader should not be able to tell, by looking at two rhyming lines, which of them came first and which was created later, for the sake of rhyme. Both lines should seem equally natural; neither should suggest that it was written just to rhyme with the *other* — even though it might very well have been. One does one's best to make each line look as though it, in and of itself, was the optimal way of packing the thought in words, and as though it came effortlessly.

A word or two now about some subtleties concerning the art of syllable-counting, and masculine and feminine rhymes. There is, in English, a class of words that float roughly halfway between monosyllabicity and bisyllabicity — words such as *higher, hire, liar, lyre, shyer, shire, quail, fail, stale, ail, phial, file, I'll, isle, loyal, oil, royal, roil, boy'll, boil, jewel, duel, cool, cruel, rural, squirrel, earl, swirl, power, tower, hour, shower,* and so forth. In different metrical contexts, these words can adapt and become either monosyllabic or bisyllabic, as needed. Accordingly, I make no apology for the fact that I have used such words to end masculine lines on certain occasions, and feminine lines on other occasions. Language is flexible, and readers need to be flexible, too. There is even one line where I use the phrase "hour after hour", and the first of the two occurrences of "hour" is closer to being monosyllabic (and hence adds just one to the line's syllable-count) while the second one is closer to being bisyllabic (and hence adds two syllables, as well as making a feminine rhyme).

I have to say, sadly, that I found myself quite turned off, when reading previous translations, by encountering scores and scores of supposed rhymes that to me were not rhymes at all. This phenomenon riddles the Elton/Briggs version to such an extent that it would be pointless to try to list examples, but to my surprise, I found that it abounds also in Arndt, who in many ways has such a keen sensitivity to sound. Thus a careful reader will stumble over dozens of false rhymes like the following ones, in Arndt's translation:

> *gently/competently, hunger/monger, passage/message, passion/expression, frack/truck, tongue/long, under/tundra, charm/swarm, islands/silence, leery/sincerely, elixir/I fear, shadow/meadow, none/on, any/nanny, tenor/manor, singer/finger, bother/mother, glance/countenance, over/cover, heed it/needed, nonce/once, revealing/feelings, travel/devil, horse/sorts, heaven/even, talons/balance, enough/off, denuded/hooded, carried/buried, hearts/part, tarry/quarry, barter/quarter, moms/comes, reward/bard, penchant/mentioned, wonders/ponders, hauteur/there, there/her, her/hear, fluster/foster, merit/spirit, lower/power, chamber/amber, consoling/lolling, hate/fête, wetting/plaiting, rigid/fidget, glamour/tremor, able/indefatigable, forgotten/trotting, another/bother, flung/throng, off/love, ruin/undoing, rambled/resembled, sense/lens, detect it/connected, tête-à-tête/magistrate, winces/princess, Onegin/begging.*

The case for the defense might simply point out that these are near-rhymes, and claim that that's all Arndt was striving for. But against this is the fact that far more of his rhymes are *real* rhymes, from which one certainly gets the impression that rhyming in the olden fashion — in Pushkin's fashion, after all! — is what Arndt was after. But for some reason, he was just willing to settle too easily for too little, in my opinion.

There is another class of non-rhymes that abounds in all the translations except for Falen's, and they are exemplified by the following, again drawn from Arndt:

> *Lyudmila/feeler, fawns/horns, balm/arm, sport/thought, really/merely, demeanor/Paulina, day does/invaders, amongst us/youngsters, born/spawn, enters/portentous, entreat us/meters, sauntered/haunted, Alina/seen her, brought us/waters, Voronskáya/aspire, far/spa, better/Benedetta, was/pause, figure/trigger, been/eighteen.*

These rhymes work, at least fairly well, in British English; however, they do not work at all in American English. Most of them (all but the final three) are based on the British dropping of the "r" sound at or near the end of a syllable. To me, such rhymes are anathema, because they do not reflect at all how I speak. In translations done by people born or bred in England, they are perfectly reasonable, but I am surprised and confused when I find — even in Falen, as American as he can be! — "honor" used as a rhyme for "Tatyana". We all have our idiosyncrasies, I guess. But I personally wouldn't touch these rhymes with a ten-foot pole.

To be sure, some of my translation's readers, even American ones, will find that some of what I pass off as rhymes (and which genuinely do work for me) don't work for them; it just goes to show that language is far more subjective than we often suppose. For example, there is one feminine rhyme in Chapter II that some readers might take exception to: that of "hamlet" with "tablet". That one, however, has its own special justification, which readers will surely pick up on.

One last apologia. Alexander Pushkin lived in an enormously sexist era, where any red-blooded author took for granted that his readers were masculine, and that in fact all "active" members of society, such as bards, bakers, and candlestick-makers, were also males. An author might well engage in man-to-man chats with his friendly reader, on such topics as *guns, guts, grog, grit,* and, of course, *girls.* This is not the way *I* write, dear reader, but if *you* can see how to make Pushkin sound like Pushkin in totally nonsexist English, then you're a better man than I! As for me, when I don my Pushkin mask, I simply have to swallow my pride as a writer of nonsexist English — indeed, as a long-term crusader for nonsexist English — and reproduce the flavor of what I am reading, for sexism was part and parcel of the culture in which Pushkin was nourished, and to fail to echo that sexism would be, well, to traduce my author–brother.

Pushkinolatry's Pipe Dream of Poetic Perfection

Speaking of reluctance to traduce one's author, I am brought back one last time to Pushkinolatry, that weird dogma at whose very core lies the tacit but utterly groundless assumption that Pushkin, being all-powerful, *never* had to compromise on words in the way that his translators do. The vision is of Pushkin picking the semantically perfect word and having the rhymes and meter just somehow work out ideally each time. Put another way, the dogma would have Pushkin totally in control of the language he was writing in, whereas the truth is that, like all the rest of us, Pushkin was partly in control and was partly pushed around by the language he was using. Even the best of bucking-bronco riders is now and then thrown, remember.

Eugene Onegin, masterpiece though it surely is, is riddled with compromises; it's just that we as readers can't see the alternative words or phrases that had this or that clear advantage over the final choice, and that therefore tugged hard at the poet's heart, but were ultimately rejected as being weaker overall. As often as not, Pushkin would find that the first word that sprang to his mind gave a trochee, not an iamb, or had too many or too few syllables, or that the perfect word to finish up a line didn't rhyme with the equally perfect word on the previous line, and so one or the other of them had to give. Compromises abound, yet even compromises can give the illusion of having fallen from heaven.

Like all of us, Pushkin encountered stone walls here and there, had to find ways around them, and had to live with compromise and imperfection; the result of his labors is a wondrous, glowing, but not flawless piece of work. Yes — dare I say it? — this novel in verse could even be *improved* here or there! This sounds like shameless blasphemy, but the fact is, it's all too easy to idolize Pushkin and to see him as being of divine inspiration, having everything work out every time in exactly the way he'd most like. But just as surely as Alexander Sergeevich erred grandly by getting lured into a fatal duel, he also erred here and there, though obviously on a smaller scale, in weaving the web of his poetry.

It is only through having an attitude of Pushkin-as-mortal, Pushkin-as-fallible, Pushkin-as-pretty-much-like-oneself, that one can approach the daunting task of translating him. Otherwise, like Nabokov, one will find oneself in a morass of self-flagellation and frustration, and one will be rapidly immobilized by what one perceives as the hopelessness of the "mathematically impossible" task. My cure for this paralyzing disease is just to remember that *poetry is not mathematics* — there is no perfection, no absolute right or wrong, no truth or falsity, no black, no white, just shades of gray. And this holds as much for the original author as for the "dainty mimics", the "paraphrasts", and the "traducers".

The Concert Pianist Who Couldn't Sight-read

Each of the many scores of stanzas that I have not memorized has nonetheless had to inhabit my brain for a good while, as I translated it. The first stage is reading it to myself a few times, trying to get its gist without help, usually having trouble with at least a line or two, often more, and then looking up all the words I don't know. The next stage is to read it over and over again to myself, probably dozens of times, and in that manner to absorb its rhythms and its sound-patterns so thoroughly that it feels totally comfortable and natural. Only then can I begin to translate it. In that final phase, there is no doubt that I know all the words and feel in genuine possession of the stanza as a whole.

When, however, I return to a stanza that I translated weeks or months ago, I am often shocked to discover that that feeling of possession was quite illusory. Words that once I thought I knew may not even seem familiar! But fortunately, a second or third go-round of this sort often solidifies my knowledge somewhat, and eventually, over months, the words enter my bloodstream and become part of me.

Do I or do I not know much Russian, then? I still have the most awful time trying to understand what people say to me, and it embarrasses me no end. Strangely, I can express myself better than I can follow others. I guess I'll just have to live with this until I've had enough experience with native speakers that in real time I can chop up the continuous slur of words that make up the seamless-seeming speech stream. Could such a pathetic speaker of Russian possibly have read and deeply understood, let alone translated, *Eugene Onegin*? Judge for yourself, is all I can say.

I remember hearing, one time, that a certain famous concert pianist had an extremely rudimentary sight-reading ability, and for that reason had a devil of a time learning any new piece — it would take him far longer than a "normal" concert pianist. But in the end, his artistry was at just as high a level as that of pianists who were fluent sight-readers, because what counted was not how *quickly* he could absorb music, but how *deeply*. What mattered was his musicianship, not his sight-readership. I would like to think that something of this general ilk applies to translation as well. Obviously, a professor of Russian is going to get into a work of Russian literature much faster than someone who merely has a second-year or third-year knowledge of the language, but what matters, when it comes to the translating crunch, is who loves the work in question, who instinctively resonates with its author and its style, and who has a way with their own native tongue. Without those, one will get nowhere — and with them, one may just get everywhere, provided one works hard.

The Saga Winds Down...

Though exhilarating in its special way, this year devoted to translating *Eugene Onegin* has nonetheless been a very lonely one. I would spend day after day largely as a hermit, having no one off of whom to bounce ideas or turns of phrase. The only person who really served as a sounding-board for my various competing alternatives was my mother, out in far California. Perhaps a couple of times a month, I would pick up the phone and read her a stanza or two, and she would give her two cents' worth on the possibilities that I'd proposed. Once in a while, she'd suggest something that was better than I'd thought of — for example, "bois'trous" in the third sonnet from the very end. I wonder if Pushkin ever asked *his* mother for advice on his choice of words? ("What say the Pushkinolatrists?", asks my mother, on this score.)

I've stated above that my main motivation for translating anything is to come into closer contact with its source — with the person behind the scenes. Although I obviously couldn't go back 170 years and meet Pushkin in the flesh, there was something I could do that had something of that magic to it, and that was to establish contact with James Falen, Pushkin's closest anglophone voice. And so first by exchange of letters, then by email, then by telephone, and finally by bodily transport through physical space (an action known as "translation" in mathematics), I got to meet Jim and Eve Falen in their natural habitat, right at the edge of a beautiful, wide lake in rural Tennessee. That first visit was several days long, and during it, I had the enormous pleasure of doing a full reading, spread out over two evenings, of Falen's translation in front of a friendly crowd at the University of Tennessee, among whom were Jim and Eve.

A few months later, I took my children down to the Falens' house to visit again for a few days, at a point when I had done perhaps 40 percent of my translation. Jim read all that there was of it at the time, chuckling now and then, and off-handedly remarked to me about a line or two, "This sounds a little as if it had been translated by Cole Porter." I could not have been more flattered, since I have adored Cole Porter's songs — lyrics and music equally — ever since I was a young boy. They're the top!

And finally, just a few weeks ago, when the translation was all done but for the tiniest final polishing brushstrokes, I once again drove down to Tennessee and spent a wonderful weekend with Jim and Eve, during which the three of us sat around their living room, this time reading *my* translation out loud, now and then comparing my version of a stanza with Jim's version (often quoted by Jim from memory), and exchanging ideas about last-minute modifications. All of this to coffee and tea, tasty chocolates, and the warmest of companionship. Чего ж вам больше?

It was on that visit, right in the Falens' house, that I did the final act of translation in this book, which was to bring Pushkin's moving dedicatory poem into English. Unexpectedly, I wound up doing it in two versions: a straight one, with Pushkin's voice, leaving it dedicated to his friend and publisher Pyotr Alexeevich Pletnyov, and another, touched up here and there so as to turn it into my own personal dedication. Both are included here.

...and the Torch Passes on

Over this past year, a marvelous torch was momentarily passed to me; by some quirk of fate, it fell to me to "be" Pushkin, just for a flash — and for that flash, I felt he was living again, somehow through me — and then it was gone, the torch was out of my hands, and Pushkin had flitted somewhere else, his soul-flame was flickering in the brain of some other susceptible soul, some other "future dunce with scant gray matter".

So here's my stab at this proud poem by Pushkin, prince of Russian bards. How dearly I'd have liked to know him, but clearly, that's not in the cards. Poor Alexander Sergeevich! "Life is", as often they say, "a bitch, and then you die." And die he did, by bullet stung. The czar got rid of Pushkin through a rigged-up duel with d'Anthès, toyer with Pushkin's wife. To save his face he gave his life, did A.S.P. Yes, fate is cruel. His voice, though stilled at tragic age, still sings upon this magic stage.

> *And thus, EO, you're finally finished;*
> *This bullet I must bite, I know.*
> *So be it, but I feel diminished*
> *For through you, I've long fought off woe.*
> *I'm grateful for the many pleasures,*
> *The pangs, the sweet and sour treasures,*
> *The hue, the cry, the feasts, the glee —*
> *For all, for all you've given me.*
> *My thanks are yours. By you attended*
> *Through calm and crush, life's crazy quilt*
> *I've savored — yes, and to the hilt!*
> *Enough. My sails are bright and mended,*
> *So off I push for unkent brine,*
> *And take my leave from Pushkin mine.*

Pétri de vanité il avait encore plus de cette espèce d'orgueil qui fait avouer avec la même indifférence les bonnes comme les mauvaises actions, suite d'un sentiment de supériorité, peut-être imaginaire.[*]

(Tiré d'une lettre particulière)

•

Not aiming to amuse the folk in
The haughty set, but just my friends,
I'd hoped to tender you a token
More worthy of the mingled trends
That make your soul so captivating,
So rife with sacred dreams, and with
Such clear poetic life, pulsating
With noble thought and humble myth;
Oh, well... With your discriminating
Fine hand, please take my chapters eight —
Half-droll, half-sad, at times romantic,
They're down-to-earth and ne'er pedantic,
These careless fruits I've born of late —
My sleepless nights' bright inspirations,
Through callow and through fading years,
My mind's detached, cool observations,
My heart's sad words, distilled from tears.[*]

•

Anxious to live, eager to feel.
— Prince Vyázemsky•

"MY UNCLE, matchless moral model,•
When deathly ill, learned how to make
His friends respect him, bow and coddle —
Of all his ploys, that takes the cake.
To others, this might teach a lesson;
But Lord above, I'd feel such stress in
Having to sit there night and day,
Daring not once to step away.
Plus, I'd say, it's hypocritical
To keep the half-dead's spirits bright,
To plump his pillows till they're right,
Fetch his pills with tears veridical —
Yet in secret to wish and sigh,
'Hurry, dear Uncle, up and die!'"

1.

So ran a rakehell's thoughts, disjointed,
Thick in the dust of trotting steeds.

2. By Zeus, by Jove, he'd been appointed
Heir to his kinfolk's trusts and deeds.
Fans of Ruslán and of Lyudmíla:•
Meet my new book! I'll now reveal a
Few things about its motley crew.
First let me introduce to you
Onegin, my true friend and trusty,
Who by the Neva's banks was born,
Just as were you, I would have sworn,
Dear reader — but my memory's rusty.
There once throve I, but left, I fear;
The North was, shall I say, "severe".•

Once his father'd been most dutiful;
Now, though, lived by the phrase "Owe debts!"

3. Still, he staged grand balls quite beautiful,
Till his creditors cast their *nyet's.*
Fate intervened to save our hero:
First Madame (of whom we know zero),
And then Monsieur, to guide Eugene.
The lad was frisky, never mean.
The Frenchman *sans un sou* — an abbot —
So as not to torment the boy,
Used games for teaching as his ploy.
Moral redress was not his habit;
At boyish pranks he'd barely bark,
And strolled his charge through Letny Park.•

When finally came youth's grand upheaval —
That age of pangs and sighs galore

4. When one is crushed on some coeval —
Monsieur l'abbé was shown the door.
Eugene thus sipped from freedom's phial;
Coiffed suavely in the latest style,
Our dapper London ladies' man
Surveyed, at last, the world's vast plan.
En français he efficaciously
Talked up a storm, and wrote as well;
Danced the mazurka like a swell,
Spinning fast and bowing graciously.
What more to want? The world, in short,
Ruled him a warm and witty sort.

5.
We've all absorbed, by candles burning,
A jot of this, a tad of that.
So thank the Lord, to shine in learning
In our old land is quite old hat.
Onegin, in the public's rating
(A court that's most discriminating),
Was deemed a bright, if stuffy, chap.
Among the feathers in his cap
Was that of, with few hesitations,
Ad-libbing glibly as a book,
And, with a connoisseur's sage look,
Remaining mum in disputations.
Last but not least, with crackling quips
He'd coax quick smiles to ladies' lips.

6.
De gustibus non disputandum
Has lost cachet, for Latin's dead;
Yet shown a Latin phrase at random,
Eugene could tell you what it said;
He'd carve the meat from Juvenal's* gristle,
Conclude with *Vale* an epistle,
And knew by heart, though slightly skew,
Aeneid verses — one or two.
He lacked the yen to go out poking
Into the dusty lives of yore —
Historic details made him snore;
But as for anecdotes and joking —
Droll tales from Romulus till now —
He'd stocked a pile behind his brow.

7.
Onegin wasn't strongly driven
Life to forsake for sake of verse.
He couldn't (though to help we'd striven)
An iamb tell from its reverse.
Theocritus* and Homer spurning,
Instead to Adam Smith oft turning,
He studied economics hard,
To learn to judge in which regard
A country's prone to be imperial,
What it might profit from, and why
It might, despite no gold, get by,
Provided it's got raw material.
His father thought this all was Greek,
And sold his farmlands up the creek.

My leisure I shan't spend on scrawling
Lists of Onegin's treasured skills;

8.   I'll say, though, that his highest calling,
His truest art, his deepest thrills,
Since early youth his keenest pleasure —
And toil and torment, for good measure —
What occupied each day his droll
And lazy, melancholy soul,
Was the science of tender passion
Or "Art of Love", in Naso's• song,
For which he, Ovid, suffered long,
Ending his days bold, bright, and brash in
Harsh exile on Moldavia's plains,
Morose and Romesick, racked with pains.

[9]•

Eugene from greenest youth dissembled.
His hopes he'd cache, he'd feign to yearn,

10.   Then dash her hopes. Oh, how she trembled!
He'd make believe that he was stern,
Standoffish, jealous, proud, obedient,
Alert — whatever seemed expedient!
So languidly his tongue he'd mute,
Or else such tongues of flame he'd shoot
Across each nonchalant love letter!
He breathed but love, he loved but love,
And lost himself in quest thereof!
A tender glance he'd flash — or better,
Bashful or bold; and yes, my dears,
Could twist that faucet of his tears!

A young girl's rapture he could heighten
By feigning this was all so new;

11.   With pre-prepared despair he'd frighten,
Or dish out flatt'ry — true, untrue.
He'd seize that moment when she'd soften,
And youth's defenses he could often
Deflect with deftest rapier wit.
He'd wait till they'd caressed a bit,
Then wring from her a meek confession
Just when he sensed her heaving breast.
Pursuing love with boundless zest,
He'd orchestrate a secret session
And then, in silence, just with her,
Give petting lessons till she'd purr.

Chapter I

12.

Eugene from greenest youth would trouble
The hardened hearts of cool coquettes,
And when, for fun, he'd blast to rubble
Some rival chap (with no regrets),
How wildly would Eugene malign him!
And with what nets would he entwine him!
But you, you blesséd husbands, you
Stayed friendly with him, through and through.
Crafty bridegrooms curried his favor
As if they'd studied with Faublas;•
And codgers, fearing some *faux pas*;
And cuckolds — friends of their depraver! —
So very smug about their lives,
About their suppers, and their wives.

[13–14]

15.

He'd still be sleeping, on occasion,
When served by servants with the post.
"Hallo? What's this? Some invitation?
Not one, but three would be my host?
Let's see — some ball, some children's party..."
Where will he dash, my dashing hearty?
Where to begin? It's all the same —
He'll make all three! Life's such a game!
But now in morning garb he's dressing,
Dons his *bolivar*,• downs his bread.
To Nevsky Prospect• now he'll head,
And there he'll stroll with nothing pressing,
Until his timepiece chimes away
For suppertime: Watchful Bréguet!•

16.

It's dark by now: Eugene steps lightly
Into his chaise. "Away! Away!"
His beaver collar glistens brightly
With frozen dust: a white display.
Talón's• his goal, where he's expecting
Kavérin;• there they'll be connecting.
He saunters in; corks fly about,
And Comet wine's• soon gushing out.
A bloody *rosbif*'s placed before him;
Truffles, fit for a youthful queen,
The finest flow'r of French cuisine;
Famed Strasbourg pie, with great decorum;
And smelly Limburg cheese (too old),
And *ananas* — sweet juicy gold.

17.
The cutlets' grease to counterbalance,
More goblets are required by thirst;
Bréguet, though (watch of many talents!),
Cries out "Ballet!" — and that comes first.
Fickle friend of dance and theater
(Take an actress — first he'd be at her
Beck and call, but then change his mind),
Our citizen-at-large behind
The scenes, he's now *dans le théâtre*
(I mean Eugene). All wait, slack-jawed.
At *entrechats* they'll soon applaud,
And hiss at Phèdre, Cléopâtre,
Recall Moïna• (after all,
There's but one goal: to wow the hall).

18.
O magic realm! Long gone's the season
When boldly flashed upon your scene
Freedom's and satire's friend, Fonvízin,•
And that lame copycat, Knyazhnín.
Ózerov basked there in spontaneous
Tears and cheers — praise simultaneous
For Semyónova's well-played part.
Katénin there revived the art
Of old Corneille, that star tragedian.
'Twas there Didelot was crowned in fame;
There, too, a sharp-tongue learned his game:
Our Shakhovskóy, that tart comedian.
And there, behind the scenes, backstage,
My youth unfolded, page by page.

19.
Where — nay, who — are you, my goddesses?
Hear my lament: Have you changed name?
Haven't strangers donned your bodices,
Nearly the same, yet not the same?
Will I once more enjoy your singing?
Will Russian stages yet be bringing
Terpsíchore's• bright soulful flight?
Or should my eyes not seek the sight,
On this dull stage, of favored faces,
And having scanned, with glum lorgnette,
This alien crowd and alien set,
Should I, depressed from questing graces,
Abandon hope, in silence yawn,
And face the truth: what's gone is gone?

20.
The crowd's arrived; the boxes dazzle.
On the parterre's a swarming roar.
The gallery's clapping, nerves a-frazzle.
The curtain, rustling, starts to soar.
Resplendent, poised for take-off, waiting
For magic strings' reverberating,
Surrounded by her corps of sprites,
Stands Istómina,• sight of sights.
Balancing on one foot alone, her
Other she slowly lifts and twirls...
A leap! She's off! She drifts and whirls,
As if the god of winds had blown her.
She twists and untwists, fleet as fleet,
Feet flutt'ring to the music's beat.

21.
Applause breaks out. Onegin enters
And seeks his seat while trampling feet,
Then points his twin lorgnette, and centers
His gaze on ladies yet to meet.
The house's every tier surveying,
He finds the faces, clothes, dismaying;
He's frightfully dissatisfied.
Politely turning side to side,
He bows to fellow top-hat strutters;
He's bored, he fidgets off and on;
He fights but can't suppress a yawn.
"Oh, for a change of scene," he mutters;
"For years I've put up with ballet,
But now Didelot seems dull and gray."

22.
Meanwhile cupids, imps, eerie serpents
Still on stage make highjinks and whirrs;
Meanwhile cohorts of weary servants
Take naps in hallways on their furs;
Meanwhile the crowd is stamping, yapping,
Nose-blowing, coughing, hissing, clapping;
Meanwhile lanterns, indoors and out,
Scatter their sparkle all about;
Meanwhile the steeds grow colder, number,
Champing restlessly at the bit;
Meanwhile coachmen, by fires half-lit,
Rub palms, curse masters, dream of summer...
But here's Onegin, out the door —
He's homeward-bound, to change once more.

23. Shall I try letting words paint pictures,
So you might see the hidden room
Wherein this slave to fashion's strictures
Would dress, undress, redress, and groom?
Whatever London sells to buyers
Abroad, to meet their hearts' desires,
Then ships, in trade for wax and staves,
Across the Baltic's choppy waves —
Whatever Paris taste's effulgence,
On sniffing out some business lead,
Invents for pleasure or for greed,
For luxury, for self-indulgence —
It's in his room. Ah, my Eugene —
Fop philosopher, aged eighteen.

24. Amber pipes imported from Turkey,
Bronze and china — whatever asks
The pampered taste, soft, spoiled, and quirky...
Sweet perfumes in cut-crystal flasks,
Numberless brushes (more than thirty)
For teeth and nails, bitten or dirty,
Scissors of straight and curvy styles,
Plenty of combs and steel nail-files.
Jean-Jacques Rousseau (I'll state in passing)
Could not see how the lofty Grimm•
Dared clean his nails in front of him,
Great silver-tongue deserving sassing;
Though he'd lit rights' and freedom's spark,
In this case, he quite missed the mark.

25. Nothing says that high ability
Must preclude pretty fingernails.
Fight the times? Why, that's futility —
Custom, timeless despot, prevails.
Eugene, Chadáyev's• second coming,
Afraid of envy's ruthless drumming,
Toed the line, when it came to clothes:
A dandy, he — yes, one of those.
I refer to that urban genus
Whose members love the looking-glass.
Leaving his boudoir, he could pass
As cousin to bright flighty Venus
Bedecked in pants, for masquerades,
Or... for venereal escapades.

26. His suave toilette, chic and discerning,
Has served me well — I've got you hooked;
So now I'll tell the world of learning
Just how our dapper dresser looked.
Though bold, 'twould be no indiscretion,
For I'm a wordsmith by profession.
Still, *pantalons, frac,* and *gilet*
Are foreign loan-words, sad to say.
In shame, indeed, my *cœur lyrique*
Regrets what issues from my plume:
It's lame in style; 'twould fairer bloom
Sans this or that *fleur exotique.*
Once, way back when, how hard I tried:
My bible, then? *The Slav's Word Guide.* •

27. But this, of course, is not our focus:
The ball's the topic we should opt
For — for, directly toward that locus,
In hired coach, Onegin's hopped.
Along the darkened street now sleeping,
The coach's double beams go sweeping,
In front of rows of flats, on snow.
The play of colors forms a glow —
A rainbow, which new snow's romancing.
And here's a splendid house all bright
Whose lampions sparkle in the night;
On all its panes there's shadow-dancing:
Let's watch, in profile, silhouettes
Of jack-a-dandies near coquettes.

28. Our hero's pulled up at the entry.
Swift as an arrow through the air,
Up marble stairs, right past the sentry,
He flies, then smooths his ruffled hair,
And steps inside. The hall is jumping;
The orchestra, though bored, keeps thumping.
Here the mazurka's drawn a crowd,
And everywhere, it's tight and loud.
Suave cavaliers flash spurs that jangle;
And flashy belles flash fleshy feet,
While men's eyes flash along in heat
And hunger, tracking each sweet angle.
The fiddles' scritch-scratch soon subverts
The fickle chit-chat of the flirts.

29.
Back when I knew joys and frustrations,
Balls made me giddy, through and through:
No better place for declarations
Or passing ardent *billets doux.*
So take, please, husbands most respected,
Advice on which I've long reflected.
I urge you, give my words a chance:
Well-meant warnings, served in advance.
And you, young mothers, you who gave us
Sweet buds of girlhood — clasp them tight!
Don't let them wander from your sight!
For otherwise... I pray, God save us!
And why, you ask, write this herein?
Because I long since ceased to sin.

30.
Alas, in fripp'ry light and trifling
I've frittered much of life away.
Take balls — for moral growth, they're stifling;
If not, I'd love them still today.
I love youth's frenzy and its bluster,
Its joy, its ardor, and its luster,
And ladies' fancy, frilly clothes;
I love their limbs, though I'd suppose
You'll find in Russia three or fewer
Well-tapered pairs of ladies' legs.
But there's one special pair that plagues
My suff'ring soul... Ach! Though mature
And sadder now, I can't forget;
In dreams, they bring me heartaches yet.

31.
Where and when, in what desolation,
O fool, will they forsake your head?
Where are you, feet, where in creation?
What flowers of springtime do you tread?
Conceived and bred in far-off places —
The blissful east — you left no traces
Upon our bitter northern snows.
You loved to feel, between your toes,
A deep plush rug or silken textile.
Did yesteryear I, in your name,
Renounce my thirst for praise and fame,
Forget my country and my exile?
Youth's joys have fled without a trace,
As from the fields your step's light grace.

32.

Diana's breast has charms enduring,
And Flora's* cheek, friends. Yet to me,
I can't say why, but more alluring
The thigh is, of Terpsíchore.
Suggestive, to the eye, of treasure,
Of higher joy, of boundless pleasure,
Its graceful curving form inspires
A surging swarm of sharp desires.
O friend Elvina,* I admire,
Near table legs, girls' hidden knees,
Cavorting calves on spring's green leas,
Cute toes in winter, lit by fire,
Feet dancing on a smooth parquet,
Or rockbound, splashed by surf and spray.

33.

I recall some storm-brewing ocean:
Jealous, I watched its waves that beat
A path straight toward her in devotion,
To swirl in sequence at her feet.
To join those waves my soul was burning,
To touch those limbs with lips so yearning.
Not once, not once in all my days
Of youthful ardor's seething blaze
Ever did I endure such anguish,
Craving to kiss Armida's* lips,
Her rose-flamed cheeks, the very tips
Of both her breasts, and feel them languish...
Not even then was my young heart
Ever so sharply torn apart.

34.

Ah, now my memory's getting stirred up:
In secret dreams, some other day,
I'm holding someone's lucky stirrup;
Her ankle lures my fingers' play...
Once more my fantasies start swarming,
Once more my heart, once touched, starts warming;
My wilting core refills with blood:
Once more she's mare, once more I'm stud!
But stop! Why should my babbling lyre
Waste words on all these haughty dames?
They don't deserve the raging flames
Or raving songs that they inspire.
These sorceresses' words and eyes —
And, yes, their limbs! — are naught but lies.

35. What, though, of my Eugene? Unsteady,
He droops, then bolts from ball to bed;
But restless Petersburg already
Hears drums announcing night is dead.
The peddler's up, the merchant's lathered,
The hansoms at their stand have gathered.
With jar, an Ókhta° milkmaid goes,
Crunching the morning's fresh new snows.
With pleasant sounds the day's thus breaking.
Shutters open, while chimneys high
Spew azure smoke-wisps toward the sky.
The paper-hatted German's baking,
And selling through his door's top half,
Which we call *vas-is-das*° (don't laugh!).

36. But bored by boist'rous balls, and spreading
His nights from morn till well past tea,
Our *enfant* spoiled by featherbedding
Now snores in sinful luxury.
Long gone is lunch when he arises,
All set for life with few surprises,
Diversified yet uniform:
A suite of days without a storm.
But was he filled in ample measure,
In this, the flow'ring of his years,
By freedom or sweet victory's cheers,
By all his constant, mundane pleasure?
Did thus our party boy exhaust
Himself in games, at zero cost?

37. Ach, no! His feelings cooled off early.
At social whirls he'd tend to snore;
A debutante, a dolled-up girlie
Arrived to haunt his dreams no more.
Addictive once, now duping faded,
And friends were dropped; how he'd grown jaded!
All this because he couldn't find
A balm to soothe his troubled mind,
Albeit steaks, cakes, drinks came staggered
At cyclic hours. Not even wit
Assuaged his sorry soul one bit;
And though he was a dashing blackguard,
All lust he quickly lost for swords,
And bullets, rifles, duelling lords.

Onegin's illness was no tumor;
Indeed, still no one's found its cause.

38. It's England's "spleen", it's our ill humor —
Our word's *khandrá,*• and in its claws
Eugene was gripped, little by little.
He didn't have the spunk or spittle
To shoot himself (the Lord be blessed),
But through and through he felt depressed.
Like Childe Harold,• spoiled and weary,
When at salons, he fast dismissed
The maidens' sighs, the games of whist,
The latest blab, and even cheery
Salutes from friends. Not taking note
Of this or that, he stayed remote.

[39–41]

Eccentric belles of high society!
He dropped you at an early stage.

42. How come? Façades of high propriety
Are tedious in this day and age.
Perchance among you someone's reading
Bentham and Say,• say, but high breeding
In general tends to make one preach
Naïve yet vapid high-flown speech.
Moreover, belles, you're all so very
Majestic, flawless, pure, and bright,
So highly holy and upright,
So fine and dainty, yet so wary,
So cool to men that once you're seen,
They suffer sudden surging spleen.•

And you, young tarts, fresh, poised, and charming,
Who ride in droshkies swift and swank

43. Till late at night beside disarming
Gay blades along the Neva's bank,
Eugene forsook you no less slowly.
Rejecting carnal pleasures wholly,
Onegin squirreled himself away
In hopes the muse might swing his way
And charm his pen — but yawns soon started,
Since writing's long and wondrous hard.
He turned out not to be a bard,
And didn't join that fiery-hearted
Grand guild of folks whom I'll not judge —
For arm in arm with them I trudge.

Chapter I   ➤➤ *13*

44.
And once again toward sloth inclining,
Languishing in his empty soul,
He took a seat and tried designing
A course of learning — worthy goal!
Off shelves he snatched a proud detachment
Of books and read — with no attachment.
Here it raved, was dull or confused,
Lacked sense; Eugene was unenthused.
Here were multifarious fetters;
The Old grew older by the page,
The New just aped some olden age.
As belles he'd dropped, he dropped belle-letters,
And o'er that dusty, learnéd crowd
He drew a cloth — a mourning shroud.

45.
We both spurned custom like the plague; in
Sharing contempt, we found a bond;
And thus I liked Eugene Onegin,
And of his features grew most fond:
His tendency toward wishful dreaming,
His strangeness, strangely normal-seeming,
His frisky, lively, piercing mind.
Where I was gruff, he was resigned.
Though once with love inebriated,
By life we both had been rebuffed;
In both our hearts, love's flames were snuffed.
For both of us, disgrace awaited:
With Fortune blind, and with men's eyes.•
So young were we, and so unwise.

46.
No one who's lived and known reflection
Could help but scorn the human host.
No one who's sampled life's complexion
Could fail to fear his dead past's ghost.
For him, life's lost its fascination;
Suff'ring pangs of self-condemnation,
He tastes the fangs of memory's snake.
Of course such traits will often make
For charm in casual conversation.
At first Onegin's caustic tongue
Dismayed me, but with time I swung
Around. His style of disputation
Oft made me smile, as did his wit,
Half-gloom, half-bile. Oh, how he'd twit!

47.
How often, in the months postvernal,
When bright and sparkling glowed the sky
Above the Neva's waves nocturnal,
We watched its glassy waters try
But fail to give the moon's reflection,
And gushing to our recollection
Came summer tales from yesteryear,
Along with ancient loves so dear
That, swooning o'er the night's sweet breathing,
We drank in silence on a spree,
Just like some sleepy refugee
From jail awak'ning to a seething
Green jungle scene, and thus through dreams
We two reswam our lives' first streams.

48.
Eugene leaned on a granite railing,
His thoughtful soul lost in regret;
Just so, some bard, in verse detailing
Himself, once penned a terse quartet.•
The nighttime's hush was barely broken
By words by watchguards rarely spoken.
The trotting droshkies'• distant beat
Echoed from Milyónnaya Street.
And drifting down the dreamy river
A rowboat, gently bobbing, rowed.
A song in some exotic mode
And far-off horns set hearts aquiver.
Despite such lures, my soul inclines
To songs that stem from Tasso's• lines.

49.
Waves of the splendid Adriatic,
O Brenta!• Soon I'll see your shores.
Inspired anew, fulfilled, ecstatic,
I'll hear that siren song of yours,
The voice Apollo's sons admire;
Through Byron's Albionic lyre•
I know it well; it's dear to me.
On golden eves in Italy
I'll drown myself in bliss by boating
With some Venetian fair and young,
Who'll talk at times, then hold her tongue,
Like some sweet sphinx. As we go floating
In gondola, her lips will teach
Me Eros's and Petrarch's• speech.

Is this the time to slip my tether?
"Indeed it is!" I shrilly cry.

50. I stroll the strand,* I spy the weather,
I wildly wave as ships glide by.
In cloak of storm, with breakers clashing,
I'll start my flight for freedom, splashing
Into the wat'ry main — but when?
It's time I fled this fearful fen,
Its hostile plain and dismal sandscape,
In search of Africa's blue sky;*
In southern ripples, with a sigh,
I'd pine for Russia's gloomy landscape;
It's there I loved and lost my mind;
It's there I left my heart behind.

Eugene and I were both preparing
To roam and share the world's strange sights,

51. When suddenly, by fates uncaring,
Our plans were shot, for such delights:
His father upped and kicked the bucket.
And poor Eugene, by sheer bad luck, it
Seemed, had gained a passel of debts,
With every lender issuing threats.
To sidestep suits and lawyers' hassle,
Contented with his current lot,
He ceded them his father's plot,
Not saddened that he'd tossed his castle —
Or had he sensed (here I surmise)
His uncle's imminent demise?

Indeed, an aide soon came, relating
A piece of news both fresh and sad:

52. His uncle lay in bed, awaiting
His fate, and hoped to see the lad.
Once he'd absorbed this dire epistle,
Onegin shot off like a missile
Upon swift postal horses' backs.
Succumbing soon to yawn attacks,
He schemed (as he was sweetly dreaming
Of cash) just how he'd sigh and stage
Fond hugs (recall my book's first page);
But when, to uncle's bedside streaming
He'd come, he found a stark white sheet
Wrapped 'round a gift for worms to eat.

53.
The manor teemed with aides funereal:
Near to the dear deceased were found
Enthusiasts for any burial,
And friends and foes from all around.
A sermon first, and next, interment;
Then feasts for priests and guests — such ferment!
They took their leave with furrowed brows
And secret smirks despite deep bows.
So here's Onegin, country squire,
Once sloppy profligate — but now,
Distillery and stream and plow
And briar and woods are his entire
Domain to run; he's glad, to boot,
His trip at least has born some fruit.

54.
For two full days he felt untroubled,
Pleased by the newness of his goods:
The river, as it purled and bubbled,
Secluded meadows, cool dark woods.
But by day three, grove, hill, and fields
Had lost their pow'r as boredom-shields,
Instead evoking just his yawn;
He clearly saw, from this point on,
That rural's just like urban boredom,
Though lacking palaces and streets,
Cards and balls and iambic beats.
From every side, malaise came toward him,
Dragging darkness into his life,
Like shadow — or like faithful wife.

55.
By contrast, I was born for plushness,
For peaceful living on the land;
Out here, one's lyric voice gains lushness,
One's dreams are sparked beyond the bland.
I give myself to harmless leisure,
And roam lost lakes with boundless pleasure;
Dolc'è far niente!* — I decree.
I wake each morning feeling free
To bask in bliss and loaf in clover;
I scarcely read, I sleep till two,
And fickle fame I'd fain eschew.
Did I not thus, in years long over,
In idleness and shadow, laze
Away my life's most joyful days?

56. Idyllic idling, blossom-smelling,
Woods, meads — you're nectar to this bee,
E'er glad to run across some telling
Distinction 'twixt Eugene and me,
So that no flippant, fearless reader
Or printing press's peerless leader
Known for his tattling slander-blat,
Noting we share in this or that,
Repeats some infamous gossip-bull,
Claiming my hero's portrait's mine
(*À la* Byron — a self-design),
As if, these days, 'twere impossible
Rhymes to write on anything but
One's two-bit self — one stupid rut!

57. And, by the way, just for good measure:
With dreamy love we bards are friends.
Once, pretty maids would bring me pleasure
By dancing through my dreamer's lens;
My mind would grasp their forms, deflate them,
Then let my muse reanimate them.
To captives of the wild Salghir,•
My fair Circassian• without peer,
I, carefree, doled out praise undying.
From you, my friends who like things clear,
Oft flies this question, quoted here:
"Oh, come now — who's behind your sighing?
Come tell of whom, in your vast crowd
Of jealous maids, your lyre's most proud?

58. Whose gaze once pressed you toward obsession?
Who pestered you, caressed your chest,
Requesting songs from crazed possession?
To whom's your reverent verse addressed?"
Well, friends, you've guessed it: No one, truly.
My quest to fathom love's unruly
Dark ocean left me sad and stressed.
But bless'd are those who've best expressed
Love's woes in rhymes compressed, thus doubling
The poet's mad, celestial zest,
As did Petrarca, at his crest,
To soothe his breast, which love was troubling,
And wresting meanwhile glory's plum;
Love's test I failed, though — deaf and dumb.

59.
Love passed, my muse appeared, and nary
A cloud remained to roil my mind.
Now freed, I seek once more to marry
Sense, sounds, and soul, through magic twined.
I write; my heart's not melancholy;
My pen forgets my former folly:
It doesn't sketch girls' heads and limbs
Near half-baked drafts of lyric whims.
No more do stamped-out ashes flare up,
And though I'm sad, my tears are dry;
Soon, soon the shards of storms gone by
Will be too dull, my soul to tear up.
Then shall I start to scrawl a terse
(Twenty-five–canto) work in verse.

60.
About its structure I've been brooding —
Its hero, how he'll be yclept;
But meanwhile, look — I'm just concluding
My novel's Chapter One. I've kept
My eye alert to weak depictions,
And noticed scores of contradictions;
I'll leave them, though, with no regret.
To censorship I'll pay my debt.
I'll hand reviewers, who'll devour,
Fresh-fallen fruits of pen and ink.
Fly bravely now to Neva's brink,
My newborn opus, fly and flower,
And earn me glory's just deserts:
Hot air, vain noise, faint praise that hurts.

Chapter Two

O rus!
— Horace

O Rus'!•

1.
They bored Onegin past all measure,
These woodlands, though a charming spot.
A friend of innocent, sweet pleasure
Might well thank Heaven for this plot.
The lonely manor found protection
From wind in hills, and in reflection
It danced upon the brook below.
The distant meadows' blurry glow
Was gold from untold blooms collected.
Far hamlets glistened through the air,
And flocks sought pasture here and there.
A garden, grand but long neglected,
Was choked with weeds grown thick and tight:
Fine shelter for a dreamy sprite.

2.
The stately manse had been erected
As manses ought to be: to last.
'Twas solid, tranquil, well-protected:
A tasteful tribute to the past.
The rooms were high and overawing,
And in the drawing-room, some drawing —
Tsarina, tsar — graced every tall
And plushly damask-covered wall.
The ovens featured flow'ry tiles.
Although this sounds passé today,
The reason why, I can't quite say.
At any rate, to all such styles
The squire was equally undrawn:
At old rooms, new rooms, he'd just yawn.

3.

He chose to sleep where his old gnarled
Late kin for forty years, it's said,
With his concierge Anísya quarreled,
Admired the view, and smashed flies dead.
The simple room had nothing broken,
No spots on walls or floor (all oaken),
Two closets, table, stuffed divan.
Onegin made a closet scan;
In one, he found bills tabulated;
The other had a brandy rack,
Tall pitcher full of applejack,
And calendar twelve years outdated:
Old uncle's days had been so booked,
In other books he'd never looked.

4.

Alone among his new possessions,
And just to pass the time of day,
Eugene drew up a few concessions
To launch auspiciously his stay.
Indeed, our idle rural sage's
First thought was that his servants' wages
Could pay their rent — a lighter yoke
Than old-time chores. They blessed this stroke
Of friendly fate. Meanwhile, some wily
And thrifty neighbor, on his farm,
Got wind of this and cried alarm;
Another neighbor snickered slyly,
And with one voice, all gave the word:
"The chap's a strange and dangerous bird."

5.

At first they'd all gone gladly calling;
But his behavior, soon they found,
Was absolutely crude and galling.
When he would hear them rolling 'round,
A-rattling down the road in flimsy
Contraptions, he would, out of whimsy,
Command a serf to fetch his steed —
A Don-bred stallion, pedigreed —
From in the rear, and off he'd hasten...
"He's mad, I say — saw him decline
To kiss a lady's hand." "And wine
He merely *sips*, the damn freemason!"
"He won't say 'sir' and 'ma'am', like us —
He puts on airs!" And then they'd cuss.

Chapter II

6.
Around that time, another squire
Returned by horse to his own green,
Inducing neighbors to inquire
As keenly as about Eugene.
"Vladímir Lensky", he was known as;
In Göttingen he'd lately grown as
A poet and a fan of Kant.
He was a handsome young savant,
And from the depths of German hoar-mist
He brought wise acorns that he'd squirreled,
Grand dreams of freedom for the world.
This fiery spirit, nonconformist,
Adored with words to shadowbox,
And sported long black curly locks.

7.
Still young, still waiting to succumb to
Life's icy ravages and stress,
His soul would warm to, purr and hum to,
A friend's hello, a maid's caress.
In matters of the heart still virgin,
With hope the lad began to burgeon,
And all the world's bright lights and noise
Still thrilled his mind — still just a boy's.
His heart had always had a leaning
Toward doubt; he calmed it with sweet dreams.
He knew life's far from what it seems
And so he sought its goal and meaning.
Thus miracles he tried to find —
He had a hunch they lurked behind.

8.
He thought there was a soul-mate fated
To be entwined with him till death;
That long for him in faith she'd waited
In sadness, yet with bated breath.
He thought his friends too true to wrestle
With fear in smashing gossip's vessel;
He thought, to save his name from stains,
His friends would bravely suffer chains.
He thought there was, by fates elected,
A ring of sacred friends of Man;
That rays from their immortal clan
Someday would shine on us, collected,
And bathe our lives in blesséd light,
A gift from poetry's sole might.

9.

In childhood, pity, indignation,
The love of Good in purest strains,
And glory's bittersweet sensation
Had caused hot fire to course his veins.
Beneath the skies of Goethe and Schiller
And with a lyre in place of tiller,
He sailed; by their poetic flame
His soul was touched. Nor did he shame
The muses of the most exalted
Of all the arts, for he was blest,
And proudly in his songs expressed
But feelings from the highest vaulted
Reaches of heaven: virgin dreams,
The charm of grand yet simple themes.

10.

He sang of love, to love deferring,
And when he sang, it rang as clear
As thoughts to artless maids occurring,
As dreams of babes, as moon's bright sphere
In heaven's tranquil vastness flying,
Goddess of secrets and soft sighing;
He sang of sadness and farewells,
Of "this-and-that" and "gloomy dells",
Of roses (how romantic-seeming!);
He also sang of far-off lands
Where long, on lonely silent strands,
His bitter tears had oft come streaming;
He sang of how life's petals fall,
This bud of but eighteen — that's all.

11.

Now in this wasteland where Yevgeny
Alone might savor all his skill,
He found his neighbors so inane he
Consumed their food as if 'twere swill,
And did his best to flee the clatter
Of all their down-to-earth farm chatter
About their kennels, pigs, and wine,
About their hayrigs, kin, and kine.
Of course their talk was short on feeling,
Nor did it glow with lyric flames,
Nor deep insights, nor verbal games,
Nor with the art of social dealing;
Their wives, though, talked — plump bovine pearls —
Still more like swine than their fine earls.

12.
Young Lensky, rich and quite a charmer,
Was everywhere sought as a groom —
Such is the custom of the farmer.
This "German Russian", he was whom
Each family'd have their daughter marry.
If he dropped by, they wouldn't tarry
To drop an ill-hid hint or two
That bachelors seldom bill and coo;
They'd lead their neighbor to the kettle,
Where Dunya'd tip the samovar;
They'd add, "She even plays guitar!"
And then dear Dunya'd show her mettle
By warbling (save us, Lord, from doom!),
"Come hither, to my golden room!"

13.
Vladímir, on the other hand, was
In no hurry for wedding bands,
But, thinking closer friendship grand, was
Glad Eugene lived near, to shake hands
With. Thus they met like prose and lyre,
Like cliff and wave, like ice and fire,
And yet they shared a few traits, still.
Though friendship's winds at first blew ill
Because of all their mismatched facets,
Things slowly warmed; each day they'd go
On horseback, and — what do you know? —
Quite soon they found each other assets.
Thus merely sharing boredom tends,
I'd say, to make two strangers friends.

14.
But friendship's not like that, in our case.
We smash all preconceptions, since
Another's face means nil, but our face
Has all the hallmarks of a prince —
Or better yet, Napoleon's features.
Those featherless bipedal creatures•
That number millions are our tools;
We laugh at how they feel, poor fools.
Eugene was gentler, though, than many.
Although, of course, he held in scorn
Most folks he knew of woman born,
There were exceptions (since to any
Rule some exist); and these, it seemed,
Though strange to him, he still esteemed.

15.
He saw Vladímir as amusing:
The poet's bent for fiery talk,
His mind, which found the world confusing,
His gaze, perfused by gape and gawk —
This all was new to old Onegin;
He felt like pulling Lensky's leg in
A mocking jest, yet was held back
By musing, "Stupid to attack
When bliss and joy he's briefly tasting;
He'll suffer plenty as he grows
Without my barbs, Lord only knows.
Just let him live, for time's a-wasting.
Yes, let him think the world's a ball;
Forgive the boy his fire and gall."

16.
Each topic triggered disputations
Between the two, and made them muse:
Pacts among dead civilizations;
Evil, good; scientific views;
Prejudices that last for ages;
Predestined secrets of sin's wages;
And fate and life; on each in turn
Their thoughtful minds would chew and churn.
The poet lent his rapt attention
To reading, meanwhile, flush with love,
Some Russian verse (or scraps thereof)
Out loud; Eugene, with condescension,
Would try to understand each word,
Though most of them he found absurd.

17.
More often, though, what captured our
Two hermits' minds was passions' flow.
Having escaped their seething power,
Eugene described them with a glow,
Yet not quite squelching sighs of sadness.
Oh, blest are those who tame such madness
And, in the end, leave it behind;
More blest are those to passions blind,
Who cool their love through separation,
Their enmity through speech that rends;
Who often yawn with wife and friends,
Untouched by jealous agitation;
Who shield late grandpa's wealth from raids
By that damn gambling deuce of spades.

Chapter II

18. When once we've hoist the flag of aging
Rational men of mind serene,
And once the flame's been snuffed of raging
Passion (amen!), our old routine
Seems quaint and droll: those stubborn yearnings,
Those outbursts, and those mid-life churnings.
Though it took time, at last we're tame;
We savor now a gentler game:
Vicarious pangs of youthful tension,
For oft they'll touch our very core.
Just so, a grizzled man of war
Will crane his neck with rapt attention
To hear tales told, in his small shack,
By front-line johnnies just marched back.

19. By contrast, flaming youth would bare its
Most private soul; deceit's too coy,
For youth is always keen to share its
Pet hates and crushes, grief and joy.
Himself as love-scarred warrior counting,
Onegin listened, and with mounting
Involvement, as the bard expressed
Himself — indeed, his life confessed;
He trustingly revealed his hunger:
His secret longings, how he yearned.
Eugene thus effortlessly learned
About the romance of his younger
Confrère, to whom 'twas all so new —
But reader, not to me or you.

20. Oh, how he loved — 'twas in a fashion
One sees no more these days; indeed,
It takes a poet's half-mad passion —
But then, such love is guaranteed.
Each moment and each place, his dreaming
Renewed itself; desires were teeming,
Each time the same, as was his pain.
Nothing could change his soul's refrain —
Not the chilling of separation,
Nor the tearing of years apart,
The hours devoted to his art,
Some fresh new beauty's sharp temptation,
A jolly feast, or learning's joy —
None snuffed the flames that fired the boy.

21.
When first he entered adolescence,
And still from love's keen dart was free,
He watched, with growing incandescence,
Her girlish games, and charmed was he.
Beneath an oak grove's shadows straying,
He joined her in her guileless playing,
And soon their neighbor–fathers said
Their children would, when grown, be wed.
Thus in a humble tree-lined alley,
Olga — untouched, unharmed, unwise,
Unspoilt — before her parents' eyes,
Shot up: a lily of the valley,
Well hid amongst the grass and trees,
Unseen by butterflies and bees.

22.
She gave him his first intimations
Of just what raptures life might hide;
His lyric flute's first exultations
Were sparked by thoughts of her as bride.
Farewell, though, golden games of childhood!
He soon preferred the deep, dense, wild wood,•
Its quiet nights with stars far-strewn,
Its lonely silence, and its moon —
The moon, that bright lamp of the night-skies,
To which we dedicate not just
Dark evening strolls, but we entrust
Our tears, sweet balm for secret night-cries;
And yet we see in her these days
A mere stand-in for lanterns' rays.

23.
Respectful, modest, ornamental,
Bright like a morn that's known no strife,
Soft as a kiss, all sweet and gentle,
And simple as a poet's life,
With azure eyes like heaven gleaming,
And flaxen curls, a broad smile beaming —
'Twas Olga's all: grace, figure, voice...
But take a novel of your choice;
Her portrait sure you'll find, enjoying
A central role therein — how nice!
I too once found it full of spice,
But these days find it bland and cloying.
And thus I'd try, if you'll allow,
To paint her older sister now.

Chapter II

24.

"Tatyana" — thus they called her sister.
The first to grace a tender tale
With this old name, I'm no resister
To names that others might find stale. •
Why not? It's pleasant and warm-sounding.
I realize I risk confounding
My readers, who'll envision dust
And chambermaids. Alas, we must
Confess we lack sophistication
And taste in names (and as for verse,
There's little doubt we're even worse).
We don't take well to education:
It's left us with a vapid core
Of affectation — nothing more.

25.

And so, "Tatyana" she was christened.
Her sister's fair good looks she lacked:
Her cheeks were pale and scarcely glistened;
Few were the eyes hers might attract.
Untamed, unsmiling, introverted,
Shy like a doe in woods deserted,
She seemed, when with her kinfolk, wrong,
As if she didn't quite belong.
Around her parents she was wary
Instead of warm, and she held back
When children gamboled in a pack,
Preferring staying solitary.
From morn till eve, she'd oft sit still,
Just brooding by her windowsill.

26.

Her truest friend was contemplation;
Since cradle days this had been so,
And dreaming was her sole salvation
From rural torpor's boring flow.
Her fingers never sewed — too menial;
Embroid'ry, slightly more congenial,
Was still rebuffed; through linens fine
She wove no ornate silk design.
Most girls enjoy the sense of power
They get from teaching dolls about
The world's fine manners, and they'll spout
Most pompously, hour after hour,
The things that just the other day
They heard their scolding mothers say.

27.
But dolls were never Tanya's passion,
Not even at an early age;
In chats with dolls on news or fashion
She made no effort to engage.
And childish pranks seemed even stranger
To Tanya's mind; but tales of danger
On darkest nights in wintertime —
Now those, indeed, she found sublime!
And when their nanny brought together
A group of Olga's friends to play,
Tatyana always stayed away
While they cavorted on the heather.
She found them dull, and chose to shun
Their laughs, their shouts, their flighty fun.

28.
When on the terrace she stood waiting
For dawn's arrival, she would thrill;
She'd watch the star-choir dissipating,
As just the palest glow would fill
The lower sky, where earth meets heaven,
And soon enough, soft winds would leaven
The atmosphere, and day would break.
In winter, when night's shade would take
Possession of one half the planet
For extra hours, and lazy east
Would loll in sleep for time increased
Beneath that hazy horn of granite —
Tatyana, every morn the same,
Would wake and rise by candleflame.

29.
From early on, she read romances;
True life they were for her, not show.
She fell for all the moods and trances
Induced by authors like Rousseau
And Richardson.● A friendly fellow,
Her father was old-fashioned, mellow,
And saw in books no cause for dread;
Instead, because he never read,
He thought of them as dull and boring,
And didn't give a tinker's damn
What brand of frivolous flim-flam
His daughter clutched all night while snoring.
But on the other hand, his wife
Thought Richardson the spice of life.

30. Richardson was her favorite writer,
But not in that she'd read his books,
Nor that she thought Lovelace[*] was slighter
Than Grandison[*] in heart, mind, looks —
But rather that her Moscow cousin,
Princess Alína, lo a dozen
If not two dozen years gone by,
Had always praised him to the sky.
Back then she was engaged already,
Though not to him for whom she sighed,
But to the man whose blushing bride
She'd soon become — a fate less heady
Than dressing up and playing cards
With "Grandison" — her Prince of Guards.

31. Like him, she was a flashy dresser
Who strove to stay in stunning style.
Her kin, though, didn't ask or guess her
Desires — just marched her down the aisle.
Her brand-new mate, to ease her grieving,
Quite sensibly arranged for leaving
The city for his farm, where she,
Among God knows what company,
Was ever pining, ever crying.
She very nearly left her spouse,
But then took charge of serfs and house:
This grew on her; soon ceased her sighing.
Thus habit from on high's assigned:
It brings no joy, but peace of mind.[*]

32. Soon habit had assuaged her suff'ring —
A trick that nothing else had turned.
One last discovery capped the buff'ring
Against whatever stung or burned.
To be precise, 'twixt work and leisure,
She came across a secret treasure:
The keys to keep her mate in line;
From that point on, her life went fine.
About the farm she oft meandered,
Paid bills, packed vegetables in salt;
Shaved serfs whose work she found at fault.
On sabbaths, soapy baths were standard.
When mad, she'd beat her maids and bark,
But kept her husband in the dark.

33.
In blood she'd used to sign (the practice,
In albums, of girls of sixteen);
She'd talked in singsong, like some actress,
And called Praskóvya "sweet Pauline";
She'd squeezed her skirts to strangulation;
She'd spoken "n"'s with affectation —
The nasal sound they use in French;
But marriage made her wife, not wench:
Corsets, albums, Princess Alína,
Her file of sentimental verse —
All these she soon forgot; and worse,
"Akúlka" now she dubbed Selína.
The nadir of this voyage down?
Her nightcap and her quilted gown.

34.
Her mate, though, loved his wife most dearly,
And let her life be her design;
He trusted her in all, or nearly,
And just in gown would drink and dine.
Thus peacefully his life went coasting.
Oft of an evening, they'd be hosting,
From down the road, some lively folk,
Informal friends, with whom they'd joke
And tell tall tales till tingling laughter
Turned gripe and gossip; time thus flew.
They'd ask of Olga, "Dear, would you
Please fix us tea?", and soon thereafter
They'd sup and all would go to bed,
Once from the farmstead guests had fled.

35.
Their household had an old tradition:
Respect for customs from the land.
Each Shrovetide, thus, 'twas a condition
That Russian pancakes be on hand.
They spent two days a year in fasting,
Loved carrousels, and fortune-casting
With folksongs,• and the choral dance.
Each Pentecost, a yawning trance
They'd suffer, while priests' words rang hollow;
Three tears they'd shed (and maybe pray)
Upon a buttercup bouquet.•
Like we breathe air, rye beer• they'd swallow;
And at their table, plates were brought
To guests by rank, as they'd been taught.

36. Thus gracefully they both grew older.
Eventually the time came 'round
When Death arrived to tap his shoulder
And bid him welcome underground.
He died just after morning's labors,
And soon was mourned by all his neighbors,
His children, and his loyal wife,
As one more pure than most in life.
He was a good and simple baron,
And on the spot where lie his bones,
His gravestone solemnly intones:
"A humble sinner, Dmítry Larin,
Lord's faithful slave, and brigadier:
Eternal rest may he have here."

37. Come back at last to his old hamlet,
Vladímir Lensky felt he must
Go see his neighbor's humble tablet
And with a sigh salute his dust.
At length he stood there and reflected;
"Poor Yorick!", then he said, dejected.
"How oft he held me in his arm...
How oft, when young, I held that charm
He won in the Ochákov action.•
He promised Olga's hand to me,
And wondered, 'Will I live to see...?'"
Then, filled with sadness and distraction,
Vladímir sat right down with plume
To write some verse to grace his tomb.

38. And there he, on the stark, dark marker
Atop his parents' graves, shed tears,
And praised their ashes — darker, starker.
Alas, life reaps too fast its years;
All flesh is grass.• Each generation,
At heaven's hidden motivation,
Arises, blooms, and falls from grace;
Another quickly takes its place.
And thus our race, rash and impetuous,
Ascends and has its day, then raves
And hastens toward ancestral graves.
All too soon, death's sting will get to us;
Aye, how our children's children rush
And push us from this world's sweet crush.

But meanwhile, friends, drink of it deeply,
Life's lightly lilting heady brew!

39. I know full well that life comes cheaply:
That's why I'm little drawn thereto.
I've closed my eyes to haunting specters,
But sometimes hope, still flick'ring, hectors
My helpless heart in some soft place.
Without the least, most fleeting trace
I'd hate to leave this world behind me;
I live and write not for applause;
Esteemed by few, I'd swoon with cause
If for my words the world enshrined me —
If, like a friend, some phrase I'd penned
Kept my soul-flame lit without end,

And rang, in someone's heart, not hollow...
Perchance, were it embraced by fate,

40. The waves of Lethe* wouldn't swallow
Some stanza I've composed of late;
Perchance (and here myself I flatter)
Some future dunce with scant gray matter
Will spy my portrait, point, and say,
"They don't make bards like *him,* today!"
Accept my grateful salutations,
Admirer of the muses' strains,
O you whose mem'ry still retains
Odd remnants of my light creations,
Whose loving hand runs gently o'er
The laurels of this bard of yore.

Chapter Three

Elle était fille, elle était amoureuse.
— Malfilâtre[*]

1.

"What next? Ah me, these crazy poets!"
"Regrets, Onegin — I must leave."
"I wouldn't hold you back. And so it's
Another jaunt — but where, each eve?"
"The Larins' place." "Now that's quite curious.
Forgive, but is it not injurious
To kill one's every night that way?"
"Not in the slightest." "You don't say!
From here, I see it all so clearly,
So tell me if my vision's true:
A simple Russian family who
Would welcome guests and strangers cheerily,
With jams and chit-chat — standard fluff
On rain and flax, plus stockyard stuff."

2.

"What's wrong with that? Me, I'd be grateful."
"The boredom — that's what's wrong, good sir."
"To me, your stylish clique is hateful;
A homey hearth I'd far prefer,
Where —" "Spare me, please, of your bucolic
Old homilies, my melancholic
Young friend, for heaven's sake, I pray!
You're leaving... Blast! But, Lensky, say —
I've grown a yen to see, from closer,
This Phyllis twin[*] — she who'd inspire
One's dreams and tears, and yes, one's lyre...
I'd meet her!" "Oh, you're joking!" "No, sir."
"My pleasure." "When, though?" "Why not now?
They'd make us feel at home, I vow.

Away!" And off they galloped quickly,
Arriving soon. There, much as in

3. Archaic days — at times too thickly —
Attention flowed and hemmed them in.
A custom first was thrust upon them:
Assiettes were served with jams crammed on them,
And yet one spoonlet served them all!
(A backwoods host can scarce enthrall
An after-dinner crowd with dances...)
As maids pranced primly, swiftly out
And crammed the doorjambs, stared in doubt
At this new neighbor's striking stances,
A courtyardful of local folks
Assessed their steeds with snorts and pokes.

The friends now end their pleasant eve's stop,
And take the shortest route back home.

4. And you and I, friends, why not eavesdrop
On idle chit-chat in the gloam?
"What's up, Onegin? Why the yawning?"
"Just habit, Lensky." "Well, it's dawning
On me that you were bored." "Not so.
But look — how dark! The sun's so low...
Come on, let's gallop fast, Andryushka!
These stupid boondocks! By the way,
Old Lárina, though slow, I'd say,
Is quite a pip in her babushka.•
My sole complaint's her berry juice —
I'm turning quite a scary puce...

But tell me: which one was Tatyana?"
"The silent, sad one, sitting still,

5. As if Zhukóvsky's 'sweet Svetlana'•
Were brooding by the windowsill."
"How come the one you love's the younger?"
"What of it?" "Well, my friend, I'd hunger
More for her sister, if, like you,
I were a poet. I'd not woo
That lifeless Olga, that madonna
By old Van Dyck. So dull's her eye,
Man, like the moon in some flat sky —
A hackneyed piece of rusticana."
The bard felt stung, gave a brusque bark,
Then held his tongue as dusk turned dark.

6.
Meanwhile, Onegin's friendly session
With all the Larins — sweet but short —
Had left on them a strong impression
And given neighbors merry sport.
Each guess would lead to other guesses;
The air was thick with no's and yes's,
With joking hints, oft wrong, oft snide,
That Tanya soon would be a bride;
And some, though blust'ring, claimed, undaunted,
The wedding date had been all set
But then had slipped since as of yet
They hadn't found the rings they wanted.
And as for Lensky — well, of course,
They'd long since fixed *his* fate, perforce.

7.
Tatyana heard and found annoying
This silly show; in secret, though,
She found herself somehow enjoying
Such thoughts' unbidden, constant flow;
Indeed, they lit a tiny fire
Inside her heart, which sparked desire;
Just so, a seed that falls to earth
Sprouts up in springtime's blaze of birth.
Her fantasy, long stirred by anguished
Aspirings to idyllic love,
Craved sweet elixirs from above.
Her heart so long lovelorn had languished,
Her breast so long had lived with none;
Her soul so longed for... well, someone...

8.
And long she longed... At last she opened
Her eyes and spoke: "My long-sought light!"
Alas, at once on *him* her hope and
Her need now focus, day and night.
Her ardent, lonely dreams are filled with
His grace; her world seems deep-instilled with
His face's magic power. And when
Some kindly maid plays mother hen,
Chirping, cooing, nursing her treasure,
Tatyana's cross. She's plunged in gloom.
When guests arrive, she starts to fume,
Resenting all their carefree leisure:
The way they turn up, just like that,
And stay and stay, to chew the fat.

Chapter III

9. And now, with keenest concentration
    She reads romantic novels through —
    And see: with just what fascination
    She sips their sly, seductive brew!
    Thanks to the happy power of dreaming,
    She brings mere ink to life, real-seeming:
    Some lad who loved Julíe Wolmár;•
    Malék-Adhél; and de Linár;
    Young Werther, in his suff'ring splendor;
    Suave Grandison, whose feats, I'd think,
    Would sweep one swift to sleep's sweet brink —
    But for our dreamer, shy and tender,
    These forms all swam as one, confused:
    Eugene is where they swarmed and fused.

10. Tasting the bliss with which she'd kiss a
    Paladin in some favorite work
    (As would Delphine, Julíe, Clarissa),•
    Tatyana, deep in sylvan murk,
    Takes solo strolls with books that gull her,
    Seeking and finding blinding color —
    The secret fire that drives her dreams,
    The fruit with which her young heart teems.
    She gently sighs, internalizing
    The highs and lows of others' plights,
    And softly, as if lost, recites
    Some letter she's been memorizing,
    To someone's beau... But our white knight?
    No Grandison, be who he might.

11. In olden days, an ardent writer,
    Daubing his brush with darker tints,
    Would make his hero grand, if triter,
    Painting him as perfection's prince.
    He'd give his ever-persecuted
    Belovéd subject wits well-suited
    To facing strife, a striking face,
    And soul attuned to depth and grace.
    The hero, flushed with joy's effusion,
    With passions pure as fire and ice,
    Would gladly die in sacrifice;
    But at the novel's grand conclusion,
    Revenge is wreaked on each black hood,
    While garlands go to grace the good.

Chapter III

12.
Our minds, though, have of late turned blurry,
For morals make us hit the hay;
To vice our novel-writers scurry;
It tends, in fact, to win the day.
Poetic fables by the British•
Will make a damsel's slumber skittish,
And nowadays she'll idolize
The Vampire with the pensive eyes,
Or Melmoth, that great gloomy vagrant,
The Wand'ring Jew, or the Corsair,
Or Sbogar's enigmatic air.
Lord Byron, on a whim, cloaked flagrant
Despairing selfishness in shrouds
Of romance, doom, and somber clouds.

13.
I ask, dear friends, just where's the theme in
All this? Perchance, by heaven's will,
I'll be possessed by some new demon —
An imp who'll clog my rhyming mill.
Ignoring threats from high Apollo
(Alias Phœbus• — I hope you follow!),
I'll lower my sights to humble prose,
And then, until my sunset glows,
I'll spin a tale in olden fashion.
At base, 'twill have a simple plan:
I'll tell about a Russian clan
And do without crime's secret passion.
I'll tell of love's enchanting dreams
And lifestyles under old regimes.

14.
I'll tell about the tack that rural
Talk by elderly uncles took;
I'll tell of trysts where boy met girl
Beneath the lindens by the brook;
I'll chart their envy, separation,
And tears of reconciliation;
I'll have them fight and lose the urge,
Yet in the end their hearts I'll merge.
Ecstatic speech I'll rediscover,
And words of agitated bliss,
Which I as well, though long ere this,
On knees before some dazzling lover
Found nimbly leaping to my tongue;
But now, life's pendulum has swung.

15.

Tatyana, o my dear Tatyana!
I'm shedding tears for your despair.
You've brought your trembling fate upon a
Silver platter into his lair.
My sweet, I fear you're bound to perish,
But first, in blinding hope you'll cherish
The thought of blissful nights with him;
You'll think life's grand as well as grim,
And sip of yearning's magic poison;
To dreams you'll yield by hook or crook.
You'll spot, where'er you look, some nook
Where you and he could drink love's joys in.
And everywhere — yes, everywhere —
You'll spy your fatal tempter there.

16.

Tatyana's dogged by love's sweet anguish;
Among her flowers, sad, she strays,
When all at once she starts to languish:
Transfixed, she drops her vacant gaze.
With cheeks aflush and bosom heaving
For several moments from her grieving,
She hears a crash, and flash! she's blind;
Her breathing stops; she's lost her mind...
And high above, as night is falling,
The moon patrols the stars' parade.
Some nightingale in some dim glade
Dissolves the hush with tuneful calling.
Tatyana, tossing in her loft,
Implores her nurse in whispers soft:

17.

"I just can't sleep; the air's so tight here.
Please crack the window; sit by me."
"What's wrong?" "It's such a boring night here.
Let's talk of how things used to be."
"Well, which things, Tanya? It's been ages,
Yet once my mind was like a sage's:
My head was filled with sundry lore
Of damsels, goblins, spooks of yore.
But memories fade — it's quite uncanny.
What once you knew, you've plum forgot.
It's sad but true — a mind will rot
As youth recedes..." "Just tell me, Nanny,
About that youth you're speaking of —
When you were young, were you in love?"

Chapter III

18.
"Oh, Tanya, stop! Your picture's hazy
Of love and marriage yesteryear.
A romance would have driven crazy
Mother-in-law, the late poor dear."
"But how, if so, did e'er you marry?"
"'Twas as God willed. We didn't tarry
Back then — I met my husband when
I was thirteen, and he but ten.
For half a month matchmakers brightened
Our family's doorstep; then at last,
With Father's 'yes', my die was cast.
I cried and cried, I felt so frightened;
They sobbed, they sang, untied my braid,
And churchward led this maid, dismayed,

19.
Into a household filled with strangers...
But you're not listening, pet, to me..."
"Oh, Nanny dear, I'm sad, for dangers
Surround and scare me, can't you see?
I'm on the verge of sobbing, crying!"
"My child, you're ill; perhaps you're dying;
Have mercy please, o Lord above!
What can I fetch you, Tanya, love?
You seem so hot when I caress you —
Here's holy water; douse your curse."
"It's not an illness — you know, Nurse...
I'm just in love." "My child — God bless you!"
Then Nanny's gnarly hands in pray'r
Swept out a cross, across the air.

20.
"In love", Tatyana murmured, chanting
The words anew with fev'rish tone.
"Oh, dearest heart, you're ill — you're ranting!"
"I'm just in love — leave me alone!"
And all the while, the moon was shining,
And with its feeble rays outlining
Tatyana's graceful, pallid air,
Her flowing tears, her loosened hair —
And there, reclining in a cranny,
Before her youthful charge's eyes,
Wrapped in a jacket twice her size,
And capped with scarf, sat gray-haired Nanny.
The whole room shimmered in a trance
Beneath the moonbeams' silent dance.

21.
And while Tatyana's eyes are lighting
Upon the moon, her heart has flown;
Now all at once a spark's igniting
Inside her head. "I'd be alone —
But first, please, Nanny, pen and paper;
Let's slide my desk; I'll use this taper;
And soon I'll sleep... And so, good night."
And by the crescent moon's soft light,
Propped on her elbow, Tanya's seething
With thoughts of *him*. She writes and signs,
And in her rashly dashed-off lines
A virgin's love is clearly breathing.
The letter's done and folded well...
Tatyana! Who's it for, pray tell?

22.
Belles I've known who're inaccessible,
Pure and white as the driven snow,
Cold, repressed, and unredressable —
Who're hard to fathom as a foe.
I'm staggered by their stares, which hurt you,
And by their haughty hoar-frost virtue;
And, I admit, from them I fled
When on their brows with fear I read
This quote from Dante's gate to Hades:
"Forego all hope, ye who'd make pass", •
For love just bores this type of lass;
To scare men off delights such ladies.
Upon the Neva's bank there dwells
A bevy of these jezebels.

23.
Awash in fawning male admirers,
Yet other oddball belles I've seen,
Smugly untouched by their aspirers'
High praise and sighs, prolonged and keen.
And what, then, found I so surprising?
Despite their genteel terrorizing,
Squelching a would-be beau's shy crush,
They somehow had the knack to flush
Him out again, perhaps through pity
(Well-feigned, of course), or else, perchance,
Their artless victims they'd entrance,
Moving, in artful style, their pretty
Lips to flip a flirtatious phrase
To lure beaus back — blind moths to blaze.

Chapter III

24. How's Tanya worse than these weird wenches?
Worse, for being simple and kind,
Steering clear of insincere clenches,
Convinced she's by one dream defined?
Worse, for rejecting affectation,
For banking on sheer gut sensation?
Worse, for not having disavowed
Her trust? For being heav'n-endowed
With fantasy, imagination,
A lively will, a trenchant mind,
A brain that's stubbornly inclined,
A heart that's prone to adoration?
Can't you forgive the fact that she
Lives life with passions fierce and free?

25. Coquettes will calculate love coolly,
While Tanya's love's untrammeled, wild;
She gives herself to true love truly,
Like an uncalculating child.
Tatyana doesn't say: "Deferment
Intensifies love's tingling ferment,
And stickier makes your spider's web.
The trick's to not let tension ebb:
With pricks of hope, first tease his vanity,
Throw perplexity at his heart,
Then shoot off envy's scorching dart,
Lest pleasure turn to flat inanity,
Tempting your slave, at drop of hat,
To slip your clutches, just like that."

26. Ahead I see one source of trouble:
To save the honor of my land,
I'll have to trace a Slavic double
Of Tanya's note in Cyril's hand.•
She really knew quite little Russian;
Could hold her own in a discussion
Just barely, even with the young;
Read seldom, in her mother tongue,
Gazettes; and hence in French penned letters.
Thus let me stress, with wrinkled brow:
The Russian language, up till now,
For ladies' love, has been like fetters.
Till now, our native tongue, though proud,
The *billet doux* has not allowed.

27.

In our fair land's fair tongue, they're teaching
Fair maids to read. "Thus Hell's road's paved!"
Cry I, who'd cringe at she-hands reaching
For *Good Intentions.*• How depraved!
I ask you gentlemen, you poets,
About the softer sex... You know it's
To them that, for some sinful spree,
You've written verse clandestinely;
In front of them your hearts you've dangled...
But what about the Russian tongue?
Their mastery thereof's unsung,
And for good reason, for they've mangled
(Most cutely, I confess) its grace;
A foreign tongue serves in its place.

28.

May God forbid that at grand balls, or
Whene'er they're done, at porch desserts,
Students show up in yellow shawls, or
Academicians clad in skirts.
Like ruby lips that shrink from smiling,
To me distinctly unbeguiling
Are girls whose Russian grammar's graced
With pearls. Perchance, to my distaste,
Some generation's fresh new beauties,
Heeding our leading journals' pleas,
Will hand us grammar's cryptic keys
And scribble ditties as their duties;
But all this scarcely touches me,
E'er wedded to antiquity.

29.

Some faintly flawed articulation
Or quaintly blemished verbal flow
Still stirs excited fibrillation
Within my breast, like long ago.
I lack the strength to voice repentance:
I simply love a French-style sentence,
Like youthful sin, so soaked with glee —
Or Bogdanóvich• poetry.
Enough's enough; I'll stop my talking
And take up Tanya's letter now;
I gave my word, and yet, somehow,
Some part of me is slightly balking,
For well I know: Parny's• a bore —
His gentle style's been shown the door.

O bard of *Feasts,*• once gay, now graver,
If only you were still with me,
30.   I'd ask for an immodest favor,
Dear Baratýnski, *cher ami.*
I'd ask that in your magic fashion
You turn to song a maiden's passion
Disguised in foreign words till now.
Where are you, friend? Please come! I bow;
To you my rights I'd fain surrender.
But there, midst gloomy crags and glades,
Disinterested in accolades,
Beneath the Finnish sunsets' splendor,
Alone he strolls. Though I cajole,
My pleas can't reach his distant soul.

Tatyana's missive lies before me;
To it religiously I cling.
31.   Each time I read it, secret stormy
Sensations storm me, stir me, sting.
Who instilled in her this graciousness,
Tender, careless, strange loquaciousness?
Who taught her tongue to make no sense,
Her heart to rave with no pretense?
Such candid bubbling's sweet but risky.
Her source I cannot guess; but read
This version, pale and flat — indeed,
To what she penned as ale's to whiskey,
Or, one might say, *Freischütz*• performed
By timid fingers still unwarmed:

I write to you — my fateful hour.
There's little else I need explain.
I know it's now within your power
To crush me with your cool disdain.
If you, though, for my fragile flower
Felt but a drop of empathy,
You'd surely not abandon me.

At first I thought that I'd stay quiet:
Believe me, I would not have shown
My shame, and you'd have never known,
Had not my fantasy run riot:
I dared to hope that once a week,
Say, on our farm I'd get a peek,

If only just to hear your greeting,
To speak a word to you, and then
All day and night to think of when —
Yes, nothing else! — when we'd be meeting.
It's rumored, though, that you're remote;
Here on the land you find it dreary,
And we don't offer much of note,
Aside from being warm and cheery.

    Why did you come to see our place?
Here in our far, forgotten station,
Never would I have seen your face,
Nor known this bittersweet sensation.
Time having calmed the agitation
Of my young soul (though who's to say?),
I might have managed to discover
My love, and been a faithful lover
And loving mother; that's my way.

    Another! No, I'd stay unmated.
I'd never cede this heart of mine.
In highest courts it long was fated:
'Twas heaven's will that I be thine!
Till now, my life was just a token
That we one day would meet in faith.
You came, and I knew God had spoken.
You'll guard me till I'm but a wraith.

    By you in dreams I've been surrounded;
Your grace, although unseen, felt near,
Your face so sweet that I felt fear;
Within my soul your voice resounded
Since long ago... A dream? No, no!
You came; I had a certain feeling...
I felt all faint and flushed and reeling,
And in my mind I said: It's so!

    And was I wrong? I heard you stealing
In stealth to me, and speaking plain,
When anguished suff'rers I was healing,
Or when, in pray'r, I tried appealing
For aid to calm my raging brain.
And there and then, in that condition,
Was it not you, dear apparition,

Who through the dark flashed quietly,
Bent gently down where I was dreaming,
And then, with love from your eyes streaming,
Spoke low and brought new hope to me?
Your aim: is it to guard and cherish,
Or else to lure, that I might perish?
I'm baffled; do I stand a chance?

   Perhaps my visions are inflated:
A fledgling's dreams of grand romance.
Perhaps some other path was fated...
Well, let it be! But from this day
My future course to you is handed.
I cannot keep my tears at bay:
I need your strength. My words are candid.

   Imagine, can you? I'm alone,
There's no one here who understands me,
My very reason countermands me,
And doomed to die, I'm mute as stone.
I now must wait for your decision:
Please smile and flood my heart with light!
Or else please dash my dreams tonight,
Alas, for what they're worth: derision.

   And now I stop. I daren't read
This note, for shame; indeed, I rue it,
But trust your honor in my need,
And bravely yield myself unto it.

32.

First Tanya's moaning, then she's sighing,
As in her hands her letter quakes.
The pinkish sealing-wax is drying
Upon her tongue, which burns and aches.
Her sleepy head drops on her shoulder,
And from that shoulder, turning colder,
Slips the strap of her gauzy gown...
The moonbeams' reign is winding down
With dawn's approach. The vale is steaming:
Pale wisps of fog sail toward the sky.
The stream grows silver, and a cry
From shepherd's horn curtails all dreaming.
The world's abuzz, for morn has come,
But Tanya's barely there: she's numb.

33.

She doesn't notice dawn's arrival;
Just sits with head hung low, remote,
Nor does she press her seal's archival
Indent upon her reckless note.
But now Filípievna,• her graying
Old nanny, trundles in, while saying
To Tanya, as she serves her tea
Upon a tray, "Get up, dear me,
It's time to rise! You'll sleep no longer!
Aha — you're up, my early bird?
Last night, you scared me so... My word!
But thank the Lord, today you're stronger.
Of last night's anguish, no more trace;
A poppy's sweetness lights your face."

34.

"Ach, Nanny, please, do me a favor."
"Of course, my pet. What is it, pray?"
"Don't think... I mean, it's just... Don't waver...
But can't you see... Please don't say nay!"
"My sweet, I won't, by God I swear it!"
"This note... your grandson — could he bear it
In silence to the house of O...
You know... our neighbor... Tell him, though,
He'll be in trouble if he's tattled,
In trouble if he's mentioned me..."
"But who's the letter for, sweet pea?
These days, my mind is often rattled.
On every side, we've neighbors now;
To count them — ach, I'd not know how."

35.

"Oh, Nanny, don't be such a dimwit!"
"I'm old, though, Tanya — old, dear heart.
My reason's far outlived its limit...
And yet, I once was pretty smart —
I once could second-guess the master..."
"Oh, what care I for your dim past, or
How your memory's lost its bounce?
My letter, Nanny — that's what counts;
It's to Onegin." "Right, dear; right, dear.
Please don't be cross, my little soul,
You know, these days, I'm just not whole.
But now, what's once more made you white, dear?"
"It's really nothing, Nanny — I
Just wish you'd make your grandson fly."

36.

The day dragged by without an answer.
A new day came; still nothing yet.
All dressed since dawn, pale cheeks, taut glance, her
Patience thinning, she starts to fret.
And then comes Olga's young admirer.
"Do tell" — her mother's his inquirer —
"Your friend prefers his lonely perch?
It seems he's left us in the lurch."
Face flushing, Tanya's in a tizzy.
"He promised he'd be here today,"
Says Lensky in an offhand way,
"But mail has clearly kept him busy."
Tatyana, trembling, drops her gaze,
As if rebuked by Lensky's phrase.

37.

Soon twilight fell, and there, aglimmer,
Whistled the evening samovar;
The Chinese teapot, left to simmer,
Brewed tea while steam swirled near and far.
The kettle, tipped by Olga, trickles
Its darkish stream, whose fragrance tickles
The senses, into each small cup.
A servant boy with cream comes up.
Tatyana, though, prefers to linger
Beside the window, pensive lass,
Breathing against the chilly glass.
She traces, with a graceful finger
On fogged-up panes, a filigree
Of cherished letters: 'O' and 'E'.

38.

And all the while, her soul was aching;
Her languid eyes were filled with tears.
But now, her blood runs cold: the shaking
And rumbling noise of hoofbeats nears.
Eugene has come! "Ach!" Helter-skelter,
Tatyana seeks some safer shelter;
From porch to courtyard, through the plants,
She darts, she flies, no backward glance
Allowing now; she scampers madly
By bridges, blooming plots and leas,
Skirts the lake trail, shoots between trees,
And tramples lilac bushes badly;
Through gardens skitters toward the creek,
And tumbles panting, dazed and weak,

39. Upon a bench... "He's come! He's driven
From far! Oh, God! His judgment's grim!"
And yet her heart, by torment riven,
Retains its dream of hope, though dim.
She's trembling, sweating, growing dizzy;
She cannot hear, and thinks, "Where is he?"
But meanwhile, peasant girls in lines
Are plucking berries off their vines
While singing, choir-like, under order.
(And why the songs? Because fruit tempts
A girl's sly mouth to make attempts...
But if she sings, her song will thwart her;
Such are the ruses and the tricks
Dreamt up by farmers in the sticks!)

*   *   *

Lassie girls, my pretty girls,
Sweetheart belles, my demoiselles,
Play your tricks, my pretty chicks,
Drink your fills, my darling jills!

*

Sing with joy our secret song,
Secret songlet that enchants.
Let's entice a handsome jack
To our maidens' country dance.

*

As we lure our handsome jack,
As we spot him from afar,
Scatter swiftly, sweetheart belles,
Pelt him well with cherries-o,
Cherries and red berries-o,
Berries and red currants-o.

*

Boys, don't listen on the sly
As we sing our secret song!
Boys, don't dare to come and spy
As at girlish games we throng!

*   *   *

40.

Tatyana pays but scant attention
To what their bell-like voices sing;
Instead, she hopes for swift suspension
Of that which makes her soft heart sting,
Of that which makes her cheeks so torrid.
And yet her breast feels no less horrid,
And in her cheeks the sting's the same,
As brighter, brighter burns the flame...
Poor butterfly that's trapped, yet beating
Its trembling, iridescent wing,
Jailed by some stupid schoolboy–king;
Poor bunny caught off guard while eating,
Spotting a distant shrub's slight jerks,
A telltale sign some hunter lurks.

41.

At last she curbed her savage yearning,
From bench arose and, with a sigh,
Set off; but just as she was turning,
Who should she chance ahead to spy,
But, like some frightful shade, Onegin,
Glowering with the gaze of a pagan;
And Tanya, as if seared by flame,
Stopped dead and stood there, filled with shame.
Much though I'd love to tell you where it
All ended, reader, I've lost steam;
I've labored under this regime
So long that I'm convinced I merit
A little stroll, and then the couch.
To be continued... This I vouch.

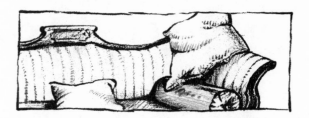

Chapter Four

La morale est dans la nature des choses.
— Necker•

[1–6]

7.
The more a girl we try ignoring,
The likelier we'll be her pet,
And certain all the more's our scoring
With her in our seductive net.
Debauchery without compliance
Was vaunted once as love's true science;
Loveless lechery far and wide
Went strutting 'round, puffed out with pride.
But this self-loving way of spending
One's seed suits monkeys from the fold
Of our great grandpas' days of old.
Of late, Lovelace's star's descending,
Just as the day has passed of big
Red heels, and of the powdered wig.

8.
Who'd not be bored by masquerading,
Saying the same thing o'er and o'er,
Doing one's best to be persuading
On points well-known since days of yore,
Always hearing the same objections,
Scorning the standard genuflections
Toward sacred cows whose folly's seen
By flippant fillies aged thirteen?
Who'd not grow tired of female rages,
Pleadings and oaths and put-on fears,
Gossip, deception, rings and tears,
Heartfelt letters of untold pages,
Aunts and mothers as chaperones,
And bonds with husbands dull as drones?

9.
Eugene was lost in just such pond'rings.
From early youth, he'd always been
A victim of his mind's wild wand'rings
And passions he could not rein in.
He suffered from a lifelong habit:
He'd see one thing and try to grab it,
Give up; for something else then strive...
And thus he slowly lost all drive,
As on him joy's brief term was dawning.
Although in silence and in din
He heard deep grumblings from within,
Yet with a laugh he stilled his yawning.
Eight years this way he killed in gloom,
Thus squand'ring life's most precious bloom.

10.
Freed finally from infatuation
With *femmes fatales,* his chase turned calm:
When spurned, he found swift consolation;
When dropped, he found the break a balm.
He chased, but never looked for magic;
He dumped, but never felt it tragic,
And fast forgot each fickle tryst,
Just like some casual player of whist.
Take you, for instance — you're arriving
For evening fun, so down you sit;
The game's now done, so off you flit,
Anticipating sleep, while driving.
Come dawn, you're still quite in the dark:
Tonight's whist host is which card shark?

Chapter IV

11.

But having gotten Tanya's letter,
Eugene was touched: it made him feel.
That girlish way in which she'd set her
Dreams as a poem, mad yet real,
Stirred up an image of her sweetness,
Her pallid bloom, her sad smile's fleetness;
And in that soft and sinless dream
He swiftly sank, as in a stream.
Perhaps some old and smold'ring feeling
Took hold of him for some brief time,
But still he knew 'twould be a crime
To lead her on, then leave her reeling...
In any case, the garden's where
We'll fly to eavesdrop on the pair.

12.

For several moments, all was quiet,
But then Eugene came up and said,
"You wrote to me; please don't deny it.
Your soul's confession I have read —
Of love an innocent outpouring,
In tone so trustingly imploring.
I value your integrity;
Indeed, it roused again in me
An ancient, dormant, yearning feeling —
But praising you is not my aim;
Instead, I'd do to you the same:
I'd tell you all, myself revealing;
So listen, please, as I confess:
'Twill fall to you, then: Damn or bless!

13.

"Were it the case that I desired
My life to stake to hearth and home;
Were it the case that fate conspired
That wife I take and never roam;
If ever, even for one second,
Myself as family man I'd reckoned —
Then surely you'd have been the one;
A better bride than you there's none.
I'll add — and not in mad regaling,
But truly — you're what once I sought,
And were I sane I swear I ought
To choose you as my mate for sailing
Life's troubled seas in search of good;
I'd be content... as best I could!

14.
"I wasn't meant, though, for such pleasure;
My soul's estranged from pleasure's call.
Vain are your virtues, far past measure;
I'm quite unworthy of them all.
Trust what my conscience makes me tell you:
Marriage to me would soon repel you.
No matter how I'd loved you once,
Once I'd grown bored, I'd start new hunts.
You'd whimper, but he who supposes
My heart would melt has got me wrong;
Instead, I'd grow enraged, ere long.
Consider thus what kind of roses
For us sweet Hymen• holds in store:
Sharp thorns, perchance forevermore.

15.
"In all this world, what's more depressing
Than families where the suff'ring wife
Is always — all alone — expressing
Despair about her married life?
And where her boring mate, despite her
Clear virtues, damns his fate? The blighter
Is always frowning, tense, and terse,
And jealous, cold, and prone to curse.
Just so am I. Were you pursuing
A life like this when with your bright
And flaming soul you chose to write
Straightforwardly, all guiles eschewing?
Is this to be your lifelong plight,
By fate predestined, out of spite?

16.
"To youth and dreams there's no returning;
I'm aging and can't start anew,
But love you as a brother, spurning
Romance; perhaps my love's more true.
So hear me out without igniting:
A girl who drifts from one exciting
Dream to another never grieves,
Just as a sapling sheds its leaves
Without regret, for spring resurges.
By Providence 'twas ever set,
And thus you'll love anew... and yet
You need to learn to tame your urges,
For few are those like me, who care —
And callow maids don't have a pray'r."

17. Eugene thus closed his well-meant preaching.
Tatyana, blinded by her tears,
And barely breathing, not beseeching,
Just listened as he clinched her fears.
He offered her his arm, and sadly
("Machinally", to translate badly),•
Tatyana leaned against him, mute,
Head bowed in shame and grief acute.
They walked home through a cherry orchard,•
Appearing arm in arm, without
Once fearing that they'd be found out
And then by ruthless gossip tortured.
Thus life out here has its finesse,
No less than in proud Moscow's press.

18. Dear reader, would you be conceding
That with poor Tanya our Eugene
Behaved himself with style and breeding?
It's not the first time that we've seen
The noble fabric of his spirit,
And yet the mob did naught but jeer it,
Which wounded him from head to toe.
Yes, each and every friend and foe
(Between the two the line's quite hazy)
Attacked him, racked him, right and left.
We're none of us of foes bereft,
But Lord, protect us from our crazy
Cabal of friends! Yes, friends, let's cheer:
For duly you're remembered here!

19. And so? Who cares? Pay no attention —
These thoughtless gloomy thoughts I'll snuff;
But *entre nous* just let me mention:
There's not a barb that's barbed enough,
Dreamt up by some depraved fanatic
Secluded in his stuffy attic
And spurred on by the craven mob,
No insult sputtered by some snob,
No trash about you that your dashing
Best friend, in chats with upright folks,
Would not (through slips, of course, or jokes)
A hundred times go gaily splashing.
He's there for you through thick and thin —
He cares for you like kith and kin!

20.
Hallo, hulloo, my gentle reader!
And how're your kinfolk, old and young?
Pray let me tell you, as your leader,
Some scuttlebutt about our tongue.
What's "kin"? It's relatively subtle,
But you'll tune in if I but scuttle:
Our kith and kin we're meant to love;
We dish out kisses, tokens of
Our high esteem; we pay a visit
Each Christmas — it's a Russian rut —
Or else send notes in greeting, but...
It isn't out of fondness, is it?
It's all so they'll forget forthwith
Us kin — and so let's toast our kith!

21.
But then again, the love of gentle
Young belles transcends friends' love, and kin's;
In tempests, though they're temperamental,
Your power to sway them always wins.
All this is true — but fashion forces;
And think of Nature's swerving courses,
The rushing tide of voguish views...
How woman's fickle — that's no news!
Moreover, any curts'ying lover
Must meet her husband's every whim —
Indulge and spoil and pamper him.
This soon grows old, as she'll discover —
And off your faithful dolly darts:
How Satan loves to toy with hearts!

22.
Whom thus to trust? And whom to treasure?
Who'll remain firm and true to form?
Who'll always most politely measure
Word, gest, and deed to meet our norm?
Who'll never slander us, or curse us?
Who with solicitude will nurse us?
Who won't be averse to our vice?
Who won't leave us bored in a trice?
World-weary seeker of some specter,
Whose search drags on and on — and how! —
Why, he whom you should worship's thou,
Who art my tale's select delector!
What wooers seek to please their heart,
Without a doubt, is that which th'art!

Chapter IV

23.

You ask, what followed from their meeting?
Alas, 'tis hardly hard to guess!
Love's bosom-wrenching aches kept eating
Away at Tanya, loading stress
Upon her soul, which courted sadness
Somehow; but now, plagued more by madness,
The poor thing's burning, filled with dread,
And even sleep deserts her bed;
Her health, her spark, her blossom also —
All perished in a sudden crash;
Her calm, her smile, turned swift to ash.
How sad to see a young soul fall so,
As when some dark gray tempest threads
A cloudless dawn with thunderheads.

24.

Whither poor Tanya? Just what's *with* her?
She's pale, withdrawn, withholds all speech.
She's without dash and in a dither;
Her withered heart's not within reach.
The neighbors all are so sagacious:
They shake their heads and whisper, "Gracious!
It's time, it's time that she were wed!"
But that's enough. It's time I sped
To lift your spirits with a pretty
Account of lovers without tears.
I just can't help myself, my dears —
I'm driven by a sense of pity.
Forgive me, but the love I feel
For my Tatyana's just so real!

25.

Ever with passing time more captured
By Olga, now quite the coquette,
Vladímir found himself enraptured
And fell into love's sticky net.
They're always one, and though they huddle
In her dark room, they daren't cuddle,
But in the garden, hand in hand,
They saunter every morn. It's grand,
And so why not? Intoxicated
By his new love, but oft bemused
By tender shame, he feels confused
By Olga's winks, and yet elated,
So sometimes he'll dare twist her curls
Or kiss her dress's hem. Ah, girls!

26. At times, to Olga he'll read stories
That teach life's lessons in the small.
The authors of these allegories
Next to Chateaubriand• stand tall.
But oft, while reading, he'll go rushing
By several pages, cheeks all flushing
(The subject matter's not for maids:
Rabid, ribald rodomontades).
Far from the madding crowd, united
Across a board, they vie at chess,
Propped on their elbows. Both sides press,
But Lensky's thoughts elsewhere have lighted.
He thinks he's moving by the book,
But takes himself in PxR.

27. His castle furnished him no respite
From dreams of Olga as his queen.
He'd take her album, and in desp'rate
Unchecked desire, would draw some scene
To grace its sheets. Perhaps he'd heed a
Whim to sketch the Shrine of Kyprida,
A gravestone, or a village view,
Or in pastels, soft green and blue,
He'd sketch a dove perched on a lyre;
Or in the part where best friends sign,
He'd make up some poetic line —
A silent keepsake of his fire,
A lasting trace of thoughts that fade,
For years preserved just as 'twas made.

28. You've surely more than once discovered
The album of some country lass,
In which her girlfriends' scribblings covered
The pages, front to back, with crass
And hackneyed verse with bumpy meter,
Words spelled so wrong they make you teeter,
Some lines too short, some lines too long,
All penned to prove the friendship's strong.
You'll find the first page somewhat pretty:
Qu'écrirez-vous sur ces tablettes?
Signed sweetly, *Toute à vous — Annette.*
And on the last page, read this ditty:
"Whoever loves you more than I
Must write hereafter; do or die!"

Chapter IV

29.
In albums, nothing's drawn so much as
A torch, a bloom, a cute twinned heart;
In albums, vows are frequent, such as
"I'm yours until death do us part."
You'll find some army bard who's flirty
Has penned some verse that's slightly dirty.
I too, my friends, I must admit,
In albums gladly scrawl a bit,
Because, deep down, my soul's persuaded
That all my verse at sense's brink
Deserves at least a nudge and wink
From knowing types, and that no jaded
Savant will ever scrutinize
My wit (or lack thereof) in lies.

30.
But you, you motley bunch of scrapbooks
From off the bookshelves down in hell,
You elegant and classic chapbooks
Who make young rhymesters fear death's knell —
You're marvelously well embellished
By Tolstoy's° brush, so widely relished,
Or else by Baratýnsky's quill —
May you burn up when Heaven's will
Makes lightning spark a conflagration!
Some beaming lady comes to me,
Extends her album hopefully;
I shake with naughty expectation,
As epigrams stir in my head —
But she'd have madrigals° instead!

31.
No madrigals is Lensky writing
In Olga's book; he'd rather dream.
His pen breathes love; thereof he's plighting;
His words with frigid wit don't gleam.
His every sensing, every sighting,
Of Olga is whereof he's writing,
And elegies whose vibrant theme
Is vivid truth gush like a stream.
Thus you, Yazýkov,° so beholden
To subtle singing in your heart,
The Lord knows whom you praise with art;
Your chain of elegies is golden,
And someday it may give, of you,
And of your fate, a faithful view.

32.

But quiet!• Don't you hear that critic
Who tells us elegíac verse
Is pap — passé and paralytic?
He'd tell our rhymester brethren worse:
"It's time you dropped your fearful croaking;
It's time sad tears you stopped evoking!
Nostalgia for the past is out;
You've so much else to sing about!"
"You're right, and surely you'll be showing
To us the dagger, mask, and horn•
By which dead thoughts will be reborn
At your behest, O Bard All-Knowing!
Not so, my friend?" "No, no! Not quite!
It's odes, good sirs, that you must write,

33.

As they were written in their heyday,
As back when they were first conceived..."
"Just solemn odes? Oh, what a gray day!
Too gray, my friend, to be believed!
Recall that play by our lampooner —
Strange Logic?• Tell me — would you sooner
Revere its hero — glib ode man —
Than be our dreary rhymesters' fan?"
"But what's in elegies is paltry;
They've empty aims and episodes,
While lofty are the aims of odes —
Aristocratic, pure, and faultfree!"
I could go on like this all night,
But won't; why pick an ancient fight?

34.

A freedom and a glory dreamer
Lost in a storm of churning thought,
He'd be an odist, would Vladímir,
But Olga would have noticed naught.
How oft do plangent poets ever
Enjoy the chance to read their clever
Creations to their lady love?
I've heard no thrill ranks thereabove.
Indeed, a modest beau's so lucky
Who gains the chance to chant his dreams
To her, the subject of his themes,
His doe-eyed beauty, pure and plucky!
He's lucky, but... for all he knows,
Her mind's adrift on distant floes.

35.
But as for me, I read the fruits of
My musings and harmonic ploys
To just my nanny, at the roots of
My precious youth and all its joys;
Or else, when some dull dinner's finished,
I grab some neighbor with diminished
Discrimination, as he's drunk,
And smother him with lyric junk;
Or else (and please suppress all chuckling),
Oppressed by poet's spleen, I take
A break to duck down to my lake,
And scare a wild drake and duckling:
They quack in literary thanks,
Then flap their wings and flee the banks.

36.
My gaze is seeking them already,•
While through the woods a hunter steals;
His trigger-finger clenched and steady,
He damns my verse and calls the teals.
Each has his own preoccupation,
Each has his favorite avocation:
One tilts arms at loons in the sky,
One finds charms in rhymes (that one's I!),
One with a swatter horseflies squishes,
One gags the crowd with laws galore,
One laughs aloud while waging war,
One basks in bed with wistful wishes,
One is a connoisseur of wine:
And Good and Evil thus entwine.

37.
But what about Eugene? Precisely!
Your patience, please, my friends, I pray.
I'll now describe for you quite nicely
Just how he passed each livelong day.
A hermit's lifestyle he was keeping;
At seven he would rise from sleeping
On summer morns and, lightly clad,
With Byron's feat in mind,• our lad
Traversed his Hellespont by swimming
Across a burbling mountain brook.
Once back, of coffee he partook
While wasting time by idly skimming
Some weak biweekly magazine.
His mode of dress had to be seen.

Ramble, nap, and book — sundry blisses;
Gurgling brook, thick woods, shade within;
39. At times, young, fresh, and languid kisses
From dark-eyed misses, fair of skin;
A steed obedient to the bridle,
A fancy feast when he fell idle,
A flask or two of sparkling wine,
Seclusion — silent, still, divine:
These were Eugene's Elysian fields,
To which he'd unawares warmed up,
Without once weighing up the cup
Of blessings filled with summer's yields.
His friends, the town, the festive grind —
All out of sight and out of mind.

And yet our fleeting northern summer
(Like southern winter, only flipped),
40. Once flashed, is gone, and leaves us glummer,
As we confess the bud's been nipped.
The sky an autumn tint had taken
And by the sun been more forsaken,
With shorter days and sharper breeze.
The murky canopies of trees
Grew sparser with sad autumn's whisper,
As fog played rug to meadows' floor.
A caravan of geese from shore
Went honking south, portending crisper
And brisker days of little charm.
November's pall had reached the farm.

Cool dawnlit fogbanks start to pinken;
In fields, the din of work's gone still;
41. Two wolves in search of quarry slink in
A roadside ditch that skirts a hill;
The coach-horse at their spoor starts snorting;
The voyager whose path they're thwarting
Goes frightened up the hill, full tilt.
A herdsman in the dawn's faint gilt
Is, out of fear, no longer bringing
His cattle from their barn; his horn
Won't summon them at end of morn;
But in a hut, a maiden's singing
And spinning yarn. A cold night's boon,
Some kindling crackles to her tune...

42.
Frost's crackling, too, but still she's cozy
Amidst the fields' light silv'ry dust...
(You're all supposing I'll write "rosy",
As Pushkin did — and so I must!)•
Slick as a dance parquet swept nicely,
The brooklet glints and glistens icily.
A joyous band of skate-shod boys
Cuts graceful ruts to rowdy noise.
A clumsy goose, by contrast, wishing
To swim upon the glassy sheet,
Lands stumbling on its red webbed feet,
And slips and tumbles. Swirling, swishing,
Gay twinkling stars — the snow's first try —
Bedaub the creekside ere they die.

43.
What do you do when cold comes roaring
Into the backwoods? Take some air?
The helpless land looks bland and boring,
Since everywhere it's been stripped bare.
Or to the steppes go horseback-riding?
Your mount with well-worn shoes goes sliding
On treach'rous ice sheets, and withal
At any time might slip and fall.
Well then, go sit beneath high ceilings
And read — here's Pradt,• here's Walter Scott.
No good? Then pay your bills — why not?
Imbibe, or work up angry feelings.
Somehow or other, day by day,
You'll while your wintertime away.

44.
Akin to Byron's spoiled Childe Harold,
In languid torpor plunged Eugene:
From bed to ice-filled bath he barreled,
And then our stay-at-home's routine
Would have him, deep in calculation,
All morning long, in isolation,
With dullish cue and just two balls
At billiards playing in his halls.
But now the country sun is setting;
His pool abandoned, cue retired,
His table set near hearth well-fired,
Onegin waits: here's Lensky, getting
Down from his troika, drawn by roans.
"Let's eat at once!", Eugene intones.

45.
Now blesséd wine is brought instanter —
Perhaps Moët, or Veuve Clicquot* —
And poured from a nice cold decanter,
In honor of the poet–beau.
It sparkles *à la* Hippocrēnē,
The Grecian muses' fountain-genie
Atop the mountain Helicon.
Its bubbling froth, in days bygone,
Quite captured me (as did some others):
For just one tiny sip I spent
My last pathetic little cent.
Its magic stream — remember, brothers? —
Gave birth to jokes and fights galore,
Gay verse, gay dreams of maids, and more.

46.
But with its fizzling froth, it tickles
The touchy lining of my gut,
And so these days, Bordeaux's what trickles
Like nectar down my throat — that's what.
Aÿ I loved but now can't handle,
For, like a lass you love to dandle,
She's sparkling, fizzy, full of spunk,
But leaves you dizzy when she's drunk,
Whilst thou, Bordeaux, art like a friend who,
No matter how one's down and out,
Is always there to share one's stout,
Always ready with hand to lend to
A friend in pain, a friend in need.
Long live Bordeaux, a friend indeed!

47.
The fire's quenched; and ash just barely
Now forms upon coal's glowing balls.
Steam, spiraling, streams up but sparely;
The hearth now hardly heats the halls.
Still fizzling stands a sparkling snifter;
From pipes, sweet smoke, an airborne drifter,
Wafts up and through, then out the flue.
(I love this time, when good friends chew
The fat, as evening's growing foggy,
And share a friendly wine or two...
In French it's *entre chien et loup*,
Which is to say, "'Twixt wolf and doggy".
I've got no notion why; do you?)
But now let's join their rendezvous:

48. "What's with the neighbor-girls? How's Tanya?
Your perky Olga — how is she?"
"Encore un demi-verre d'champagne...
Assez, mon vieux... The family
Is fine; they send their warmest wishes.
But friend, I tell you — how delicious
Have grown her shoulders — and her breasts!
And, yes, her soul... Sometime as guests
We ought to go. In fact, you owe it,
My friend, to them. Think: were you nice?
You showed your nose, months back, just twice;
Since then, you've not deigned once to show it.
Now that's... Good God, man — am I dumb!
They've asked if this week you can come."

49. "If I would come?!" "Yes — Tanya's nameday
Is Saturday. They did invite
The two of us. To spare me shame, pray,
Don't seek a pretext — be polite!"
"But man, the place will swarm with rabble
And stupid, vapid, social babble..."
"A crowd? Why, hardly — that I swear!
Just family — just a small affair.
Let's both accept — do me the favor!
What say?" "All right." "Thanks — you're high-class!"
And thereupon he tipped his glass
In honor of their nameday neighbor,
And then resumed his singing of
The charms of Olga: Such is love!

50. Ecstatic he! In but a fortnight
The blissful day was coming up,
When secrets of that ship-in-port night,
The sweetness of love's honeyed cup,
At last would all be his to savor.
But sadly, there's a side far graver
To Hymen, which makes spouses yawn,
Although on him this didn't dawn —
Whilst we who carry high the banner
Of foes of Hymen see therein
Just rows of scenes of rows and din,
In Lafontaine's• "romantic" manner...
Poor Lensky's future we must mourn,
For this is wherefore he was born.

51.

He was belov'd — at least love's fever
Convinced him this was Paradise;
Blest hundredfold's the true believer
Who, having warmed his inner ice,
Discovers peace that's heart-restoring,
Like some poor drunk who's finally snoring,
Or, softer, like a butterfly
That's sucking vernal blossoms dry.
But pity him who's all-foreseeing —
His is a head that never spins;
To him all words and acts are sins
On every level of their being;
By too much life his heart's been chilled;
His lust for life's been all but killed.

Chapter IV

Chapter Five

O, do not know these terrible dreams,
Thou, my Svetlana!
— Zhukóvsky•

1.
That year, autumnal weather hated
To take its leave from mead and dell;
The world e'er, e'er for winter waited.
'Twas January ere snow fell,
The third, by night. By dawnlight waking,
Tatyana, by her sill, was taking
The morn's white farmyard in: the sheds,
The fence, the roofs, the flowerbeds,
The glass's faint fantastic tracery,
The trees with wintry silver decked,
The court with merry magpies flecked,
The mountaintops' light lucid lacery —
Their dazzling, glistening, wintry shawl.
The air was crisp; bright white was all.

2.
Winter! A peasant's celebrating,
Driving a nag that sniffs the snow;
A fresh new track they're excavating,
Which makes their trot molasses-slow.
Nearby, a swift *kibítka*• burrows
Deep parallel and fluffy furrows,
Its driver high behind its dash
In sheepskin coat and bright-red sash.
A farmyard tyke runs out, lost mitten,
And sets his doggie on his sled;
He's then their horse (inside his head)...
This rascal's finger's soon frostbitten,
And yet he laughs despite the cold's
Sharp pangs, while housebound mama scolds.

3.

It may well be that you don't revel
In kitsch depictions of this type,
So crass, on such a low-class level,
So graceless, tasteless, such trite tripe.
A rival bard's interpretation,•
Sparked by the god of inspiration,
Brilliantly captured snow's first kiss
And every shade of winter's bliss.
He'd thrill you, friends — and this I'd swear to —
By painting with his flaming pen
Clandestine sleigh-rides o'er the fen.
But stage a contest? I'd not care to,
Neither with him, nor, bard, with you,
Whose ode paid Finland's maid her due.•

4.

Tatyana, Russian deep in spirit
(Though as to why, she had no clue),
Adored our Russian winters. Here it
Is good and cold, lovely and blue.
She loved the way the frost is sunlit,
The sleighs, the way the morning's unlit,
The rosy tint of fallen snow,
And Twelfthtide evenings' gloomy glow.
They held an old-style celebration
On all such evenings in their home,
With serf-girls gath'ring in the gloam
To reckon fates through divination:
Each year, each mistress heard with joy,
"To you will march an army boy!"

5.

Old legends struck Tatyana's fancy
As more than merely grains of truth:
She read her dreams, did cartomancy,
And tried astrology, forsooth.
All 'round were signs she found upsetting;
Some mundane sight would set her fretting,
Foretelling secretly some fact;
Her breast with cryptic hints was packed.
If on the stove some cat sat purring,
Using its paw to clean its snout,
This presaged, well beyond all doubt,
That guests were due. At once inferring
Some message from a crescent moon
In leftward skies, she'd start to swoon,

6.
Her face would blanch, her hands would quiver.
Each time a shooting star would arc
And shoot across the dark star river,
To dissipate in faintest spark —
In panic, Tanya, softly speaking,
While still her star above was streaking,
Would tell it what her heart desired.
If anywhere it so transpired
That on her way she crossed an abbot
Attired in black, she'd fall perplexed
From fear, unsure what she'd do next.
Or if across her path a rabbit
Should scamper by, the evil eye
Would haunt her, warning woe was nigh.

7.
The strange thing is, this very terror
To Tanya's breast brought secret joy.
Thus, drawn to paradox and error
Our race was fashioned — Nature's ploy.
Such glee, as Yuletide season started
And carefree youth its fortune charted,
In bloom, without regret or gloom,
Before whom life appeared to loom
An endless stretch of bright tomorrows,
While old age groped for luck or doom
Through spectacles, and glimpsed its tomb
Where all would vanish, even sorrows;
Yet old age didn't mourn or mope:
Lies spring eternal, babbling hope.

8.
With fascination, Tanya ponders
Hot sealing wax poured in a bowl,
Congealing fast as 'round it wanders,
Revealing facts for some poor soul.•
Now, one by one, each anxious daughter
Observes her ring pulled from the water,
And when they fish out Tanya's ring,
This song from olden times they sing:•
"A fortune's there for every peasant;
They shovel silver, rake in wealth.
To thee to whom we sing, good health
And fame!" Despite the ditty's pleasant
Refrain, its plaintive tune bodes ill,
While "Kitty"• makes the maidens thrill.

9.

The night is cold; the sky's transparent;
The silent choir of heaven's spheres
Flows tightly meshed, no orb aberrant.
Tatyana, loosely clad, appears
And strolls across the farm's expanses;
Her mirror tilts till moonlight dances,
But trembling in the somber glass
There's moon and moon alone, alas. *
Now hark! The snow cracks — someone's coming...
She tiptoes up on dainty feet,
Inquiring in a voice so sweet
It rivals any reed-pipe's humming:
"Your name, o stranger chanced upon?"
He stares, then answers "Agafón." *

10.

Tatyana planned for divination
That night, * as Nanny thought was best.
A bathhouse-table preparation
For two was her polite request.
But then she felt a sudden shiver —
And I, too, feel my heart aquiver,
Recalling sad Svetlana's fright... *
Let's skip this fortune-telling night.
Her silken sash Tatyana looses,
Then gets undressed and climbs in bed,
While love-god Lel* floats overhead.
Beneath her pillow, filled with goose's
Soft plumage, lies her looking-glass.
All's calmed for night; asleep's our lass.

11.

The dream she dreams is tinged with madness.
She dreams that o'er some snowy glade
She's trudging, through a mist whose sadness
And wistfulness her mood pervade.
A dark gray stream still effervescent,
Despite the winter's chill incessant,
In waves and eddies roars and churns
Through snowdrifts, everywhere she turns.
Two logs, by ice by chance stuck tightly,
Create a bridge that spans the creek,
Albeit creaky, wet, and weak.
Poor Tanya's head is spinning lightly;
She stops before the roaring brink
So as to catch her breath and think.

Chapter V

12.
As at an angry separation,
She shouts in furor at the creek,
And seeks, in utter desperation,
Some helping hand, but all is bleak.
Then all at once, a snowdrift's shifting —
Who's there? Whose head is slowly lifting?
A woolly, wild, gigantic bear
Whose howls, with Tanya's, pierce the air,
And then the beast extends a tightened
And sharp-clawed paw to her; she gasps,
But with a trembling hand she clasps
The paw and sallies forth, less frightened.
Once o'er the stream, she's up a trail,
With bear, unshaken, on her tail.

13.
Tatyana, scared to look behind her,
Steps up her pace, already swift.
She sprints, yet cannot help but find her
Pursuer's nearly closed the rift.
This frightful, loud fur servant lumbers
Along; ahead, the pinewood slumbers
In stately, melancholy grace;
Its trellis holds, in tight embrace,
A heavy snow-rug. Through the tangled
Bare tops of aspen, birch, and lime
Falls filtered starlight — faint, sublime.
The trail's run out; the blizzard's strangled
The brush and steep ravines below;
All's buried deep beneath the snow.

14.
She's reached the woods; the bear keeps tagging
Behind; the snow plays at her knees.
Now suddenly, stray twigs are snagging
Her by the neck, and branches seize
By force her golden earrings, snatching
Them from her ears. Soft snow's now catching
A sopping boot; it starts to fall
From off her foot. She drops her shawl,
And in a flash it's gone forever.
The bear's so close that she can't stem
Her fear. Too shamed to lift her hem,
She makes one final brave endeavor
To shake the beast — it's life or death —
But all in vain: she's out of breath,

15. And tumbles to the snow. There sitting,
She's seized and dragged off by the bear.
Unconscious now, to him submitting,
She neither stirs nor takes in air.
And with her, through the woods he surges
Till all at once a hut emerges,
Decrepit, overrun by brush,
And lost in snowfall's lonely crush.
A candle lights a little dormer;
Loud noise and cries meet Tanya's ear.
The bear confides: "My kin lives here;
Inside you'll be a little warmer."
He heads directly for the door,
And there he leaves her, on the floor.

16. As Tanya wakes, she's stunned, she's blinking:
A hut? No bear? Some strange mistake?
A shout is heard, some glasses clinking,
As if it were a funeral wake.
All seems to her so sense-defying...
A crack she seeks, for secret spying.
And what's to see, behind the chink?
A group of monsters drowned in drink:
A horned one with a canine muzzle,
Another with a rooster's head,
A skeleton that acts well-bred,
A bearded sorceress — watch her guzzle!
A dwarf with tail... Now there, what's that?
A cross between a crane and cat!

17. A spider next, with crab upon it...
Yet weirder, odder sights abound:
Here see a skull in scarlet bonnet
Atop a goose-neck, spinning 'round;
Here squats a windmill, wildly dancing;
Its creaky wings it waves while prancing...
Loud barks and cackles, whistles, bangs,
Strange singing, stomping — folksy twangs!
Imagine Tanya's consternation
When she espies a special guest —
The one she fears and yet loves best —
The hero of our verse narration!
Yes, midst the crowd Onegin sits,
And toward the door his coy gaze flits.

18.

He gives a sign — they all act busy;
He drinks — they drink and wildly shout;
He laughs — they laugh until they're dizzy;
He frowns — they cut their laughing out;
About who's boss, no room for error,
And Tanya, feeling far less terror —
Athirst, in fact, to find out more —
Starts gently opening the door...
At once a wind comes rushing, blowing;
The flames go out in all the lights,
Hushing the horde of household sprites;
Onegin's eyes grow fierce and glowing;
He stands and makes a thund'rous roar;
All rise; he thunders toward the door.

19.

She's struck by fear, and in a hurry
She tries to flee but sees no way;
She turns and tosses, all a-flurry,
Can't even shout, voice won't obey.
Eugene flings wide the door, revealing
The maiden to these spooks unfeeling,
These spooks from hell... A harsh guffaw
Breaks out and soon, each eye and claw,
Each crooked trunk and tufted tail,
Each whisker, tusk and fang and horn,
Each bloody tongue, all cut and torn,
Each bony finger with its nail,
Is turned toward Tanya, as they whine
And shriek and shout, "She's mine! She's mine!"

20.

"She's mine!"• exclaims Eugene with grimness;
The monsters puff into thin air;
Remaining in the freezing dimness
Are he and she, the fateful pair.
Eugene now gently pulls Tatyana
Inside, and lays her down upon a
Small wobbly bench;• but just as he
Reclines upon her breast, they see
With Olga, Lensky, without warning;
A sudden flash lights up the scene,
And having waved his arms, Eugene,
With wildly swerving eyes, starts scorning
And scolding these unbidden guests,
While Tanya's mortal terror crests.

21. A fight explodes; the cabin rumbles,
And all at once Eugene has grabbed
A long sharp knife; Vladímir crumbles
And shadows thicken; he's been stabbed!
A scream is heard; the hut starts shaking;
And Tanya wakes, scared stiff and quaking...
Aglow's her room; she's in a daze,
And through the frozen panes, pink rays
Are dancing on the walls' white paper.
As Tanya looks, the door is drawn
And Olga, bright as northern dawn,
As carefree as a swallow's caper,
Addresses her good-naturedly:
"Adrift in dreams, whom did you see?"

22. But Tanya held her silence, spurning
Her sister and, well-tucked in bed,
She read and read and kept on turning
The pages of some book, instead.
Although this book had no pretensions
To poetry's profound inventions,
To timeless truths or pictured plot,
Still nobody — not Walter Scott,
Nor Seneca, nor Baron Byron,
Nor Virgil, nor the great Racine —
Not even *Chic Modes* magazine! —
Seduced so deftly as this siren:
Martýn Zadék,• Chaldean sage:
He'll read your dream, friends — quite the rage!

23. There once had come an errant vendor
Tramping through their neck of the woods;
One opus of creative splendor
Caught Tanya's eye, among his goods.
Malvina• (though the set was broken),
Plus this, he traded for a token:
A grammar book, two Petriads,•
Three rubles and a half, plus scads
Of vulgar fables bound in leather,
As well as Marmontel (Tome III).•
Martýn Zadék soon came to be
Tatyana's favorite, and together
With him she found life gay, not grim;
Indeed, each night she slept with him.

24. Tatyana's nightmare leaves her lurching.
Unsure of what its scrambled stream
Of images might mean, she's searching
Zadék, to pierce her horrid dream.
Thanks to its index she's explored her
Fears in alphabetical order:•
Bear, blizzard, bridge, cat, crab, crane, ditch,
Ghost, hedgehog, snowstorm, stabbing, witch —
Et cetera. But her confusion,
Fueled further by Zadék, extends:
She's sure her frightful dream portends
Adventures leading to delusion.
For many days on end, she seems
Quite haunted by its gruesome themes.

25. But now Aurora's crimson fingers•
In drowsy valleys, with the sun
Behind her, melt what fog still lingers,
To usher in the nameday's fun.
From dawn, the Larin household's bustling
With guests; whole family packs come hustling
In carriages, *kibítkas,* sleighs,
And *britskas*• drawn by roans and bays.
The hallway's crammed; the crowds are jostling;
The parlor's where new faces meet,
Dogs bark, girls kiss and chirp and tweet;
There's noise and laughter, clinks and wassailing,
Deep curtseys, bows, and shuffling feet,
While nurses screech at kids that bleat.

26. Old portly Pustyakóv• came gladly,
With his old portly wife in tow;
Gvozdín, who never treated badly
His peasants, though their lot be low;
Skotínins, he and she, both graying,
Prodigious progeny displaying,
As old as thirty, young as two;
The dapper Petushkóv passed through,
As did my cousin, dear Buyánov,•
Clad gaily in a high-peaked hat
(You've seen him oft, no doubt, like that),
And just-retired advisor Flyánov,
That gossip-mongering balloon,
That bribable old rogue–buffoon.

27.
Monsieur Triquet, sharp-tongued and witty,
A glasses-wearing, red-wigged man
Who used to live in Tambov city,
Came with Panfil Harlikov's clan.
A gallant Gaul, he'd penned upon a
Small sheet a verselet for Tatyana,
Sung to a children's melody:
Réveillez-vous, belle endormie.•
Some almanac's old dog-eared pages
Contained in print this little jewel,
And, well-versed in the poets' school,
He'd dusted off the dust of ages,
And being tricky, *belle Niná*
He struck, and wrote *belle Tatianá.*

28.
The idol of the elder misses
Has come from some close army plant;
A plum for mums and sisses, this is
The grand Battalion Commandant!
In he strides, with news monumental:
We shall have music regimental!
In fact, this was the colonel's call.
There's general joy — there'll be a ball!
The girls swoon in anticipation,
But first, of course, they must have eats.
The couples, hand in hand, take seats,
With maids near Tanya near elation;
Across from them, their gentlemen.
All cross themselves, and dig in, then.

29.
The chat's now dropped and just left hanging,
So mouths can chew, and all around
The plates and silverware start banging,
Mingling with tinkling wineglass sound.
The guests quite soon, though, take a notion
To raise a wholesale loud commotion.
No one listens; many cry out,
And laugh and argue, squeal and shout.
But now the doors swing wide, and there is
Vladímir — then Eugene. "Thank God!"
The hostess cries, "But how you plod!"
The guests squeeze tight; each one with care is
Transferring plate and changing chair;
When done, they call and seat the pair.

30. It's Tanya's place they wind up facing.
As pale as moon in morning skies,
As frightened as a doe that's racing
To save its life, she casts her eyes
Straight down, to hide their blur; she's burning
Inside, from passion's fire; she's churning
And choking, feeling faint. She hears
No greetings from the friends, as tears,
Full-formed, now try to fall. She's ready,
Poor thing, to swoon from fear — and yet,
Sheer will and strength of reason get
Her through this crisis, keep her steady.
She murmurs just a word or two,
Then sits back down to eat anew.

31. Tragic, nervous, melodramatic
Comings and goings bored Eugene.
Fainting and tears he found traumatic:
Enough he'd had of this stock scene.
Surprised by such a fancy dinner,
Our oddball friend was irked. Yet, in her
Sad eyes he'd seen that frightened look,
And so, although with spleen he shook,
He hid his gaze and sulked, debating
Just how he'd best get Lensky's goat;
Ah, how revenge would let him gloat!
And now, this joy anticipating,
He started sketching, in his mind,
Caricatures of all who dined.

32. Of course, Tatyana's teary blinking
Was well in range of many eyes;
The focus of folks' looks and thinking,
However, was the rich meat pies
(Which, sad to say, were salted doubly);
And now they're bringing Russian bubbly,
Before the flan but after flesh,
In flasks that sticky pitch keeps fresh;
Then rounds of wine in fine, thin glasses
Whose shape to me recalls your waist,
Zizí,• thou crystal to my taste,
To whom trite verse I wrote in masses,
Thou vial of punch in whom I'd sunk,
In whom I drowned of love, punch-drunk.

33. *Pop!* goes the cork, just liberated
From flask's tight neck, and now the wine
Comes fizzing forth. A bit inflated,
And keen to read that last trick line,
Triquet stands up. The guests adore him,
And as they hush, afford a forum.
Tatyana's nearly swooned; Triquet,
With sheet in hand, once turned her way,
Sings out, off key. And yet he's greeted
By claps and shouts. Her duty's hard,
But Tanya curtseys to the bard,
Who plays unproud, despite praise meted.
He toasts her health before the throng,
Then nobly proffers her his song.

34. Well-meant congratulations drowned her;
Tatyana, though, thanked one and all.
However, she began to flounder,
With blushing cheeks, fatigue, and pall,
When toward Eugene the crowd was turning;
But he was touched to see her churning,
And wordlessly, he gave a bow;
Yet something in his eyes somehow
Revealed a strangely tender numen.
Now, whether he was moved in truth,
Was teasing like some flirt uncouth,
Or simply showing he was human,
In any case his gaze expressed
Some warmth, and she felt less oppressed.

35. They're shifting chairs; it makes a rumble;
They throng the drawing-room in bands;
Just so, a swarm of bees will bumble
From honeyed hive to meadowlands. •
Fulfilled from fatty, festive eating,
Each guest his fellow guests is treating
To sundry sounds that say, "I'm stuffed."
The ladies ring the hearth; the fluffed
Young damsels whisper in the corners,
Whilst green felt tables are revealed,
Which lure the codgers to the field
For games like whist, whose harshest scorners,
Despite their scorn, still know the rules.
Such boring games; such boring fools!

36.
Eight rubbers now they've finished playing,
These whiskered old whist salts; eight times
Rotated seats instead of staying —
And tea's now served. I love the chimes
That link the hours to meals (and tea-time),
And yet we country gentry, *we* time
Our days dispensing with display:
Our stomach's better than Bréguet!
(Oh — *à propos,* I'd like to mention
That every bit as oft to feasts —
To forks and corks and pork-filled beasts —
I in my stanzas draw attention
As thou, o Homer, bard divine,
Though three millennia's glory's thine!)

[37–38]

39.
The tea was served, as I was saying.
The girls had scarcely sipped at all
When sounds of winds and brasses playing
Came drifting from the next-door hall.
Abandoning his tea with rum-swirls,
The local Paris cries out, "Come, girls!"
That's Petushkóv, who loves the roar.
He ushers Olga to the floor;
Then Lensky, Tanya. Harlikóva,
A spinster-lass with too much lard,
Goes spinning with that Tambov bard;
Buyánov borrows Pustyakóva...
The dam now down, guests flood the ring;
At last the ball is in full swing.

40.
As I my tale's first sails was trimming
(Please check out Notebook Number One),
I felt that, *all'Albáni,* • limning
A northern ball would be quite fun.
But by a daydream too attracted,
In my weak way I got distracted,
Recalling charming ladies' feet.
I've had my fill, though (though 'twas sweet!),
Of rambling homages to ankles.
In style and substance I've attacked
My youth; I'll now clean up my act
Before my self-indulgence rankles,
And from my Notebook Number Five
I'll dump all dumb digressive jive. •

41. Relentless, mindless, once beginning,
Like youth's whirlwind that ne'er would die,
The noisy whirlwind waltz keeps spinning
And couples keep on flashing by.
Revenge around the corner lurking,
Eugene, who secretly is smirking,
Approaches Olga; all at once,
They're doing daunting dancing stunts
Before the crowd; when done, he seats her,
And chits and chats on this and that,
Thus killing time; then, tit for tat,
To yet another waltz he treats her.
The guests are ogling in surprise,
And Lensky can't believe his eyes.

42. A gay mazurka's now resounding.
Mazurkas once were played so loud
They left gigantic halls' walls pounding;
The floors would tremble 'neath the crowd;
The window frames would shake like thunder;
Of late, though, this old style's gone under,
And sadly, men, like ladies, glide
O'er well-waxed floors. Unturned's the tide
In countryside, however, where the
Mazurka's kept its primal charms:
Hops, heels, mustaches. Yes, on farms
It's stayed untouched, not had to bear the
Tyrannic rule of fads' tight noose,
That illness of the *nouveaux Russes.*

[43]

44. Buyánov, kindly cousin–brother,
Led Tanya to our favorite son;
Eugene, though, deftly picked the other,
As pick he must (revenge is fun).
He led her, nonchalantly gliding,
Leaned over, tenderly confiding
Some trite and vulgar phrase of praise,
And squeezed her hand — and all ablaze,
Her cheeks, as pink as fresh carnation,
Expressed her smugness; Lensky saw
It all; it stuck fast in his craw;
And so, in jealous indignation,
He waited till the band was still,
Then asked to have the last quadrille.

45. But Olga's taken. Taken!? Taken —
Already promised to that beast,
Onegin. Surely she's mistaken?
Oh God, my God — she could at least...
What nonsense, this? Just out of swaddling,
A flighty flirt, though barely toddling?
With cunning now her strongest suit,
She plays betrayal's trump, to boot!?
Thus muses Lensky, shocked and stricken.
These female tricks he starts to curse,
Stomps out, shouts "Horse!" in tones so terse
It's scary — and he's flown. Plots thicken.
Two guns, two bullets — nothing more —
Will fix two fates: One final score.

Chapter Six

Là, sotto i giorni nubilosi e brevi,
Nasce una gente a cui 'l morir non dole.
— Petrarch•

1.

Aware of Lensky's brusque departure,
Eugene, once more by boredom chased,
Twirled Olga as his thoughts grew archer:
Revenge was sweet; he liked its taste.
He yawned; then Olga yawned, while peeking
Around, in vain Vladímir seeking.
The last quadrille dragged on and on
Nightmarishly, 'twas so long-drawn —
But finally stopped for snacks at midnight.
The beds were all prepared; each guest
Was told, "The maid's room's where you'll rest",
Or "Down the hall"; then all just slid right
Beneath their quilts, for sleep serene.
Just one went home to dream — Eugene.

2.

The earth is calm; the moon is soaring;
The parlor holds stout Pustyakóv,
Who near his stouter wife is snoring.
Gvozdín, Buyánov, Petushkóv,
And Flyánov (ill from overwining)
Recline on chairs inside the dining
Salon, where rests Monsieur Triquet
In cardigan and *vieux bonnet*.
The girls in Olga's and Tatyana's
Small rooms are all embraced by sleep.
But by the window, sunk in deep
Distress, suffused with bright Diana's
Caress of light, poor Tanya stays,
And with dark eyes, dark land surveys.

3.

He'd come so late; he'd seemed her savior,
So tender, just for one brief glance;
With Olga, his bizarre behavior
Had made it seem he sought romance.
She simply could not understand him!
These scenes came flashing back at random
And pricked her soul with envy's dart,
As if cold hands had squeezed her heart,
As if below her — black, voracious —
A chasm roared and opened wide...
"I'm dying now," Tatyana cried,
"And yet to die by him were gracious.
I won't complain, my breath I'll save:
He just can't give the love I crave."

4.

But onward, onward, speeds my story,
As now a fresh new face arrives.
Five versts removed from Krasnogórie
(That's Lensky's hamlet) lives and thrives —
Yes, even now — in shy seclusion
And philosophical reclusion,
Zarétsky, once a hoodlum king,
Once kingpin of some gambling ring,
Once pothouse hound, once scoundrels' leader,
But now reformed, now straight and dry,
The single father of his fry,
An upright friend (though tenants' bleeder) —
In fact, a man by all esteemed:
Thus are our age's sins redeemed!

5.

The worldly set had spread admiring
Canards about his naughty pluck,
Such as that once, his pistol firing,
From fifty feet an ace he'd struck,
Or that in battle, as a trooper,
Uncowed, despite his drunken stupor
(Or thanks thereto), he'd shined in mud
By toppling, pie-eyed, with a thud
From off his Kalmuk steed straight into
French soldiers' hands, and through this coup
Old Regulus• was born anew,
Most nobly willing to give in to
Cuffed hands — in trade for bottles three
Each morn, on credit, *chez Véry.*•

6.
He used to joke around most drolly:
Your simpler fools he'd tease a lot,
Your clev'rer fools he'd suck in wholly,
At times covertly, others not.
Of course sometimes his cute distractions
Provoked unhoped-for back-reactions;
Of course sometimes he'd make huge gaffes,
And suffer would-be victims' laughs.
Yet jollily he stirred up squabbles
And flashed his wit and acted dumb,
At times with well-timed moments mum,
At times with well-timed senseless gobbles.
His joy was getting friends enraged —
A ploy for getting them engaged

7.
In duels; or else he'd reconcile them
And treat them to a lunch for three,
But then behind their backs defile them
By wafting lies in joking glee.
Sed alia témpora.• Bravado
Is just another callow motto
And fades with youth (like dreams of love).
Zarétsky, as I said above,
Beneath the shelter of acacias
And cherries,• left his youthful rage
Behind, to live as a true sage:
He now plants cabbage, like Horatius,•
Breeds ducks and geese, and, 'midst his trees,
Shows all his sprigs the ABC's.

8.
He wasn't stupid — nowhere near it;
And though Eugene thought him perverse
At heart, he loved Zarétsky's spirit
And insight into things diverse.
In visits they'd indulged extremely,
And so it hardly seemed unseemly
When old Zarétsky came to call
The morn that followed Tanya's ball.
But after but the briefest banter,
The latter cut right to the heart,
By proffering, on Lensky's part,
A note Onegin read instanter
While standing by the window, shocked.
Meanwhile, his friend's mean smile was locked.

9. The note was crisp, aristocratic,
A pointed challenge, or *cartel*:
Polite, clear, frigid, and emphatic,
A call to duel and fare-thee-well.
Onegin showed no sign of terror,
But staring at the missive's bearer,
Declared his gun was "Always cocked",
With words so fierce they'd not be mocked.
Zarétsky rose without objection;
He really didn't wish to stay,
For this would be a busy day,
And so walked out. Now on reflection,
And in his heart of hearts, Eugene
Felt saddened by the recent scene,

10. As well he might, for thinking clearly,
And judging for himself his act,
He blamed himself for all, or nearly:
Thus first of all, plain sense he'd lacked
In taking love just budding sweetly
And mocking it so indiscreetly;
And second: Let the poet live
And let him rave; one can forgive,
At eighteen years, such hubris — this is
The rule! Eugene, who loved the youth,
Might well have shown he was, in truth,
Not just a ball of prejudices,
Nor hothead soldier-boy — nay, nay;
But *un monsieur très distingué.* •

11. He might have shown more of his feelings,
Instead of bristling like a beast;
He might have tried more gentle dealings,
And thus defused the keg, at least.
"But now, alas, too late — it's over...",
Onegin thinks. "What's worse, moreover,
That duelist just had to pry;
That gossip — slick and glib and sly...
What should have been his taunts' exaction
From me? Mere scorn, of course, but wait —
The whispers and snide laughs I'd rate..."
We're driven by the mob's reaction!
Yes, pride's with what our mainspring's wound:
It's pride that makes our world twirl 'round!

The bard awaits at home his answer,
The while he boils with anxious bile.

12. Then comes that pompous verbal dancer,
Their neighbor, with a solemn smile.
The jealous lad starts celebrating,
To know the lout (whom now he's hating),
Though slipp'ry, hasn't weaseled out,
Through jokes or ruses, from their bout;
The zealous cad won't flout their gunrise.
The outcome's now beyond all doubt:
Tomorrow dark they'll both take route
To meet beside the mill at sunrise,
To cock their pistols, aim away
Toward thigh or temple, pull, and pray.

Having resolved to hate the cruel
Coquette, he didn't wish to run

13. The risk of meeting ere the duel,
But watched his watch and watched the sun,
And though his heart half-hoped to ban her,
Its stronger half pulled toward her manor,
So, shrugging, off he rode to find
Her sad and shame-faced, he opined —
But no such luck; as at the very
First flirtings of their fervor, she
Leapt off the porch the moment he
Flashed into view, and quite contrary
To what he'd thought, was hopeful, gay,
And merry as a lark in May.

"Why did you leave last night so early?"
Was all she asked, but all at once

14. His feelings went all soft and swirly;
Head lowered, mute, he felt a dunce.
All gone were jealousy and rancor,
For never had her face seemed franker,
More simple, tender, or more clear,
Her soul more lively or more dear!
He stares at her, all adoration,
And sees that he's still loved, of course;
Already suff'ring from remorse,
He's set to beg for exculpation.
He trembles; words come slow, thoughts fast;
He smiles; his storm has almost passed...

Once more plunged deep in thought, dejected,
Because of Olga's grace and light,
17. Vladímir doesn't feel collected
Enough to ask about last night.
Instead he thinks, "My lot's to save her.
I can't accept that this depraver,
Through fiery sighs and praise, someday
Might tempt her childlike heart to stray;
Or that that stinkworm go unscolded
For gnawing at my lily's stem;
Or that this two-day bloom, this gem,
Should wither when just half-unfolded!"
In short, my dears, this sketch he's drawn:
"My friend and I shall duel at dawn!"

If Lensky only somehow knew that
Tatyana's heart burned in distress;
18. If Tanya only had a clue that —
Or rather, if she just could guess —
That Lensky and Eugene tomorrow
Would vie for graveyard shadows' sorrow,
Perhaps her love for both her friends
Could bring them — ach! — to make amends!
But no one, either through divining
Or luck, guessed what she suffered from.
Onegin, for his part, stayed mum,
While she in secrecy was pining;
Her nanny was the last resort,
But brightness wasn't Nanny's forte.

All evening Lensky was distracted.
'Twixt taciturn and gay he flipped —
19. As one on whom our Muse has acted
Is prone to be: dark-browed, tight-lipped.
He touched the keyboard, chords essaying;
Then, after just a trace of playing,
He turned to face his youngish miss,
And whispered, "Can this be, this bliss?"
But clocks had ticked; 'twas time for quitting.
His heart grew tight from death's faint smell,
And as he bade his belle farewell,
It came within a hair of splitting.
She stared at him — her flame, her torch.
"Is something —" "No." He crossed the porch

20. To mount his stallion, homeward destined.
Once back, he gave his guns a look,
Recased them all with care, undressed and,
By candlelight, took down a book
Of favorite poetry by Schiller,
But quit, obsessed with which the killer
And which the killed would be at dawn,
Yet all the while what spurred him on
Was Olga's transcendental beauty.
He shuts the tome and grabs a plume;
His verse flows out and fills the room
With loving words, if slightly fruity,
His voice full-fraught with lyric fire,
Like drunken Delvig's* festive lyre.

21. His lines by luck were kept; let's scan some:*
"What once I was no longer I'm,
Nor will to me a second chance come:
The treasures of spring's golden time
Have leapt, unseen, right through the transom.
My future's either bleak or handsome —
But which? It lurks in fog sublime.
No matter; Fate has flawless rhyme.
Thus, should I fall to arrow's puncture,
Or should it miss and streak astray,
Tomorrow's clement,* come what may —
Come sleep, come wake, come fateful juncture!
For blest's the day, though worry thrives,
And blest's the night, for murk arrives.

22. Her sparks will Venus soon be sending;
Anew, day's light will start to loom;
While I, perhaps, shall be descending
The path to death's deep cave of gloom,
Where Lethe slow will surely swallow
All mem'ries of the bard, and hollow
Will ring his name to all except
To you, fair lass, who will have crept
Up to my urn untimely, sobbing
And thinking back: 'He loved me so;
To me alone he gave his glow,
His daybreak, stormy, sad, and throbbing.'
Dear friend, sweet friend, forfend my fate;
Come see me, your intended mate!"

23.
And on he rambled *darkly, limply,*
("Romantic" stuff, supposedly —
Though how that label fits I simply
Can't fathom — but let's let that be);
Then finally, just before Aurora,
His sleepy head went drooping for a
Brief moment, at the voguish word
"Ideal"; he then no longer stirred;
But just as sweet dreams overtook him,
His neighbor boldly strode right in
And broke the silence with his din,
Entreating Lensky as he shook him:
"Now rise and shine, for on the dot
At sev'n he'll be there, like as not!"

24.
Yet soundly as the deadest rock's doze,
Eugene was dozing as they spoke,
While Phosphor,• greeted by some cock's crows,
Dispelled night's shadows; day thus broke.
Still sleeping deeply is our squire,
Although the sun slides ever higher;
Though flurries shift and blow about
In dazzling swirls, the lazy lout
Just keeps on sleeping, sweetly sleeping —
For bed, for him, is Bed Sweet Bed.
But somehow, finally, sleep has fled;
He draws his curtain's flaps for peeping,
Surveys the sky and sees it's late;
It's time he rose to make his date.

25.
He rings; and in a trice, or faster,
Comes French valet Guillot, who throws
Fur shoes and gown before his master,
Then tenders him his underclothes.
Onegin, dressed in half a twinkling,
Requests Guillot (who'd had no inkling)
That he prepare to come along,
And bring the weapons — several strong.
The readied sleigh awaits its hateful
Half hour; Onegin hops inside.
He tells his man, once mill's been spied,
To load Lepage,• his favored fateful
Device; then, having scanned the land,
Points out two oaks where steeds should stand.

Chapter VI

26. Impatient, Lensky'd long been waiting,
Leaning against an earthen dike;
Zarétsky, meanwhile, was berating
The millstone, acting expert-like.
Arrives Onegin, with excuses;
Zarétsky balks: "But where the deuce is●
Your second, man?" In duels, he
Loved classic rules and pedantry;
For how they worked he had deep feeling;
He saw, in killing, room for play,
Though hardly in some casual way —
But to the art's strict rules appealing.
To hallowed standards he stayed true
(For which high praise from us is due).

27. "My second?", sneered with condescension
Eugene. "My friend — Monsieur Guillot.
I trust there's no cause for dissension
About my choice, from friend or foe.
Although unknown, he's wise and mellow;
You'll find him quite a stalwart fellow."
His scorn Zarétsky scarcely masked.
Eugene faced Lensky, bowed, and asked,
"Well, shall we shoot?" "Unless you're yellow..."
Spits back Vladímir, so they stride
Behind the mill, their time to bide.
Our "expert" and the "stalwart fellow",
Conferring, set *les règles du jeu,*
While friend–foes fret, *baissés les yeux.*

28. First friends, then foes! How long's the measure
Of time since bloodthirst made them split?
And how few days since they shared leisure,
And food, and food for thought, and wit,
In friendly form? But now they're callous...
Like foes who've borne each other malice
Since being born, they now prepare,
As in some senseless, weird nightmare,
A pair of traps to snare each other's
Warm beating hearts, in coldest blood.
Why can't they nip this in the bud
Ere hands are red, to part like brothers?
Why can't they laugh? Because of pride —
For shame's what foes can least abide.

29.
Lepage revolver, brightly gleaming:
A hammer clinking on a rod,
Sharp bullets into barrels reaming,
First trigger-click: an unshot wad.
A grayish powder, harmless-seeming,
Inert, upon the gunpan streaming;
A firmly screwed-in flint, all cocked;
Guillot, behind a stump, still shocked.
Foes' overcoats cast to the soil;
Zarétsky pacing, counting twice
To thirty-two, to be precise.
The enemies, once friends so loyal,
At measured stretch's furthest reach,
With mortal pistols, one shot each.

30.
"Marchez maintenant!" In ruthless stalking,
Each gun held low, each friend — each foe —
Starts pacing firmly: calm, unbalking...
Four paces taken, *quid pro quo* —
Four paces toward misfortune taken...
Eugene keeps marching, firm, unshaken,
And now he slowly, coolly lifts
Lepage; therewith the balance shifts...
Five further steps; Miss Fortune beckons,
So Lensky, squinting, sets his sight;
Too late — a bullet's just in flight —
A matter of but few split seconds,
And thus the wheel of Fate has spun.
The poet, dumbstruck, drops his gun

31.
And on his breast he gently places
His hand, then crumples to the dirt.
The foggy look upon his face is
Of death expressive, not of hurt.
Once, slowly down some sloping mountain,
Aglow as though sun's frozen fountain,
A lonely snowball fell and rolled...
Now, suddenly, Onegin's cold;
He runs, he stares, he calls — but vainly:
The youth's no more. The budding bard
Has met his destiny, ill-starred!
The bloom's turned brown, its shape ungainly,
The storm's calmed down, by light of dawn;
The altar fire, once bright, is gone.

32.
Immobile, with an undistressed tone
Expressed most strangely by his brow,
He lies, and just below his breastbone
His bleeding wound is steaming now.
To moon is odd• about such matters,
To some, perhaps — but ach! — death scatters
A human heart in so few beats:
Hopes, fears, loves, hates — all life's conceits!
How like a vacant house, his mortal
Remains, for all is murk and hush;
Forever stilled, its former rush;
Its windows white with chalk, its portal
All boarded up, its shutters shut,
Its mistress gone, for God knows what.

33.
Ah, how delicious, tartly quipping,
To rouse to rage some bungling foe;
What joy to watch him, moose-like, tipping
His clumsy antlers to and fro;
Perchance your boy will near a mirror,
And peering, see himself far clearer
Than e'er before, and burn with shame;
What fun when then he howls his name!
A tip: it's even more delightful
To dig a grave to square his slights,
To frame his forehead in your sights
At just the distance — measured, rightful;
But shooting him to Kingdom Come
Falls short of Paradise, dear chum.

34.
Suppose your friend lay dying, thanks to
A bullet issued from your gun,
For you'd been driven by his pranks to
Take issue with some things he'd done.
A smirk or quip flashed without thinking
Offended you, for you'd been drinking,
Or in a touchy mood, in spite,
He'd proudly called you out to fight...
Think: What would be your soul's condition
If, prostrate there upon the ground,
His face the face of one death-bound,
His body stiff'ning in position,
He lay there, deaf and mute as steel,
Despite your last, distraught appeal?

35.

With anguished pangs of conscience stricken,
Yet squeezing still his smoking gun,
Eugene regards his friend, too sick in
His heart to say a word. "You've won!
Cheer up — he's dead!", declares Zarétsky.
He's dead! Eugene now knows regrets he
Will never shake, so long he lives.
Then shaking terribly, he gives
A call to those who've watched the slaying,
And leaves. Zarétsky does the rest:
Loads frozen corpse in sleigh's soft nest.
His steeds smell death, and frightened, neighing,
They lick their bits with white, wet drool,
Then shoot, like arrows, from the duel.

36.

Ah me, have pity for our poet,
For in the flush of blissful hopes,
He'd hardly had the chance to sow it
When life was reaped; his precious tropes
All bit the dust before they'd flowered...
His "quiddity" — adored art thou, word,
Still sacred to Vladímir's• ghost —
His sigh-spot — whither that whole host?
Where fled his stormy love-desirings,
His thirst for sense, for lit'ral truth,
His dread of paraphrasts uncouth?
And you, his innermost aspirings,
And you, unearthly dreamt-of times,
And you, our poetaster's rhymes?

37.

Perhaps for goodness' sake, or glory's,
Vladímir Lensky, bard, was born;
His silenced lyre perchance hid stories
Untold, which through his magic horn
Blown sweetly, might have made men gladder.
Some high-ranked rung on fame's tall ladder
Perhaps awaited him. Perchance
His suff'ring shade's deep mystic dance
Lies buried with him; thus for us is
Forever lost a vibrant voice.
To thank him would have been our choice,
But our mere mortals' chants and fusses
Can't reach across death's mystic pale:
Our hymns we'd sing to no avail.

But here's a quite distinct scenario,
In which his lot's more commonplace:
39. All gone is Olga's glib Lothario,
His soul-fire but an ashen trace.
His changes — nay, his self-betrayals —
Are vast: his erstwhile Holy Grails —
The muses — they've been dumped. His life?
A comfy country one, *cum* wife.
This placid bathrobe-lounging cuckold
Learns how things are: has midlife gout,
Eats, drinks, gets bored, grows ill, turns stout,
And one fine day, with belt unbuckled,
Gives up the ghost in bed, among
His leech, his ladies, and his young.

But I'm just spinning fancies, reader;
The truth, alas, is that the bard,
40. Young lover, pensive daydream-breeder,
Was killed when with his friend he sparred!
Near to his farm, in consecration,
Near where he drew his inspiration,
Where stand two pines whose roots are twined,
Where splashing brooklets twist and wind
Until they join up, down the valley —
Here where the ancient plowman naps,
And here, where shallow water laps,
And reaper-girls fill jars, and dally —
Within this serried creekside shade
A simple monument was laid.

And there (when in the spring it's sprinkling
And rain first moistens grass and grains)
41. A shepherd braids bright fibers, crinkling
Them into sandals, to the strains
Of songs of fishing on the Volga.
Some city girl who's heard of Olga
While passing summers on the land
Rides up alone on horseback, and,
By jerking on her reins of leather,
Arrests her steed before the stone
And lifts her veil; from this high throne
She casts shy darting glances nether
And reads the simple lines, then sighs
As tears fog up her tender eyes.

42.
She rides, sunk deep in wistful dreaming,
Across the pristine mead and rill,
Her soul with thoughts of Lensky teeming
For hours on end, against her will.
She wonders: "What was Olga's fortune —
From year to year to bear the torch in
His mem'ry, or few tears to shed?
And where's her sister — still unwed?
And where's that sullen, modish loner,
The one who flees all social whirls
And modish, pretty party-girls —
The murd'rer of this tombstone's owner?"
In great detail I'll be your source
On all these matters, in due course...

43.
... but not quite yet. Although I'm spurning
My deeply loved protagonist,
Of course to him I'll be returning —
But for the nonce, Eugene's dismissed.
I'm graying, and toward prose inclining —
Gray prose — while puckish verse maligning.
Shall I confess my petty crime?
I chase the petticoats of rhyme
With less abandon than I used to.
My pen is lax — it's lost its zest
To spoil fresh virgin sheets with jest...
By life's harsh knocks I've been reduced to
A trembling soul who night and day
To nightmares and daydreams falls prey.

44.
I've known the call of alien yearning,
I've known the ache of grief's first blow;
The former's brought but hopeless churning,
While grief has aged yet not let go.
O dreams, o dreams, where's all your sweetness?
Your flower's fled with — trite rhyme — "fleetness". •
And has it finally come to be
That youth has lost its greenery?
And has it come to happen, truly,
Without fanfare or flow of tears,
That spring's flashed by, my blooming years
(As oft I'd said in sport, quite coolly),
And won't come back? Can it be so?
Can my next port be "Thirty ho!"?

45.

And so my afternoon has started;
This bullet I must bite, I guess.
Well, let it be; but let's be parted
On friendly terms, sweet youthfulness.
I'm grateful for the many pleasures,
The pangs, the sweet and sour treasures,
The hue, the cry, the feasts, the glee —
For all, for all you've given me.
My thanks are yours. By you attended
Through calm and crush, life's crazy quilt
I've savored — yes, and to the hilt!
Enough. My sails are bright and mended,
So off I set, by fresh winds borne,
To take my leave from this, my morn.

46.

Just one last look... Farewell, haunts cherished,
Where flashed my youth on far-off shores
Bestrewn with pangs and hopes that perished —
The dreams of one whose soul still soars.
And you, fresh muse of inspiration,
Please spark my numb imagination;
Please speed the slumber of my heart;
Please storm my fort more oft with art.
Let not the poet's soul now shiver,
And grow more bitter, turn to bone,
And in the end become a stone
Sunk in life's deathly drunken river —
Yes, in this flume where, with you, I
Must flounder, friends, until I die!

Chapter Seven

Moscow, Russia's beloved daughter!
Where to seek thy equal?
— Dmítriev•

How not to love Moscow, one's home?
— Baratýnsky•

"Running Moscow down! So that's what seeing the
world brings! Well then — where's it better?"
"Anywhere — anywhere that we're not."
— Griboédov•

1.
Now chased by springtime's radiant beamlets
From the encircling mountains, snow
Has raced its way in muddy streamlets
To flood the meadowlands below.
Thus Mother Nature, smiling clearly,
Salutes the year's new morning blearily.
The sparkling skies are growing blue.
The woods, which one can still see through,
Have donned a downy greenish aura.
In search of nectar in the dell,
The bee flies from its wax-walled cell.
The valleys, drying, burst with flora.
The herds are lowing; nightingales
In night's still silence sing their scales.

2.
How sad I grow on your returning,
O spring, o spring, love's time of bloom!
How sharp, how languorous the burning:
Within my blood, my soul, what gloom!
How dark and dense the tender feeling
That I enjoy, by scents sent reeling,
As past my face spring wafts its green,
In Nature's lap, calm and serene.
Or has enjoyment lost its savor,
And what once brought life's joy to me,
What once had gleamed exultantly,
Now brings ennui, a dreary flavor,
To this old soul, dead long ago,
For whom all now has lost its glow?

3.
Or do we mourn to see, resprouting,
The leaves that fell to autumn's knife,
Reminded of their bitter routing,
By harking to fresh sylvan life?
Or — could it be? — to Nature's waking
We oft compare, with spirits aching,
Our youthful years' fast-fading track,
To which there is no coming back?
Perhaps to mind a thought comes, fleeting —
A lyric image framed in sleep,
Of some far spring — a distant leap —
And sets our hearts to rapid beating,
Through dreams of far exotic sights
And wondrous, eerie, moonlit nights...

4.
At last the time has come — the season
For hedonists and lazybones,
Fledglings in Lévshin's school of reason,•
All you happy-go-lucky drones,
Rural Priams with seed o'erweening,
Ladies of sentimental leaning:
You're called by spring to country soil —
Season of buds and warmth and toil,
Strolls that kindle the sweetest longings,
Season of sensuous starlit nights.
The fields, my friends! Quick, set your sights!
In coaches jam-packed with belongings,
Drawn by old nags or postal steeds,
Flee the town and flock to the meads!

5.
You, gentle reader of my ditty,
Ensconced inside your coach sublime,
Desert the rat-race of the city,
Where you enjoyed the wintertime,
And with my temperamental muse, let's
Savor the woodland sounds and views; let's
Savor a nameless country scene
And nameless brook where my Eugene,
A hermit drifting in dejection,
Had wintered up till recently,
Beside the farm where she roamed free,
She of the dreamy predilection;
But he no longer haunts this place:
He left, and left a haunting trace.

Chapter VII

6.

Let's seek, we two, some verdant clearing
That's lost midst crags, and then a rill
That snakes through green'ry, slowly nearing
A creek that skirts a limetree hill.
Here ne'er the nightingale reposes,
But trills till dawn; here bloom wild roses.
Here sings a spring deep in a cave —
Here stands a stone above a grave
In shade of pine trees, old and knurly.
Some chiseled words tell passers-by:
"Vladímir Lensky, bard, lies nigh.
A hero's death he suffered, early,
In some sad year, at some sad age.
Rest thou in peace, o youthful sage!"

7.

Time past, above this humble coffin
A wreath hung, hinting mysteries,
Beneath a pine's bent branch, and often
It gently swayed in morning's breeze.
Time past, a pair of mourning lasses
Would come and clasp here; but time passes.
Those days, late in the afternoon,
They wept at graveside, by the moon.
These days, the grave's grown old and dreary;
It's been forgotten, and its trail
Is choked with weeds. The wreath's a nail.
These days, under the pine branch, weary,
A graying shepherd mends a pair
Of shoes, and hums a lonely air.

[8–9]

10.

My poor sad Lensky! Yes, she mourned you,
But hardly cried. So young in years,
A lass, your would-be bride soon scorned you,
Alas, betrayed her short-lived tears.
Another quickly caught her fancy;
Fawning and oozing with romance, he
Answered her needy lover's grief.
A lancer brought her sweet relief.
This handsome *uhlan** so enchants her!
Before the altar, see them stand
Beneath a wreath. She takes his hand
With modesty, her glance askance, her
Fair brow tipped down, her eyes afire
Yet shy. She smiles a smile yet shyer.

11.

My poor sad Lensky! Past life's ending,
Confined in timelessness remote,
Did the dejected bard find rending
The fateful news that she'd turned coat?
Or, lulled to sleep by Lethe's crossing,
Numbed blessedly by lethal tossing,
Is now our poet beyond all hurt,
The world to him shut off, inert?
It's true! Beyond, what's waiting for us
Is barren, void, and without end.
Voices of lover, foe, and friend
At once are quelled. A grating chorus
Of loving heirs who want their slice
Sets off a family feud. How nice!

12.

The Larin house grew sad and hollow
Too soon, when Olya's ringing voice
Was gone. Her lancer'd had to follow
His squad. Such was his lot: no choice.
Between her bouts of bitter crying,
Wishing her daughter well, and sighing,
Her mother seemed about to die.
But Tanya's eyes were strangely dry.
Her mournful countenance was covered
By death's own pale and ghastly shade.
When to the porch the family strayed
To say good-bye, and several hovered
About the pair to wave and shout,
Tatyana led their carriage out.

13.

At length she watched them go, and only
Turned her gaze when they'd turned to haze,
Leaving her all alone and lonely.
Alas! Her friend through endless days,
Her turtle dove, her little sister,
Her confidante — so soon, she missed her! —
Forever snatched by faceless fate,
Now's sundered from her childhood mate.
She wanders, shadowlike and goalless,
Stares at the empty garden, sad...
By nothing is she rendered glad.
Squelched tears don't help to make her woeless;
Relief won't come; there's naught to do...
Her grieving heart has split in two.

And in her loneliness, thoughts crowd her
And sting, as higher burns her fire.

14. First softly speaks her heart, then louder,
About Eugene, that distant squire.
He being far, she can't lay eyes on him;
Truth won't let her not despise in him
One who'd kill his brother... and hers...
The bard's now gone. His spent flame stirs
The hearts of few; he's been thrown over
Already by his promised girl.
His trace has vanished, like a curl
Of smoke that's swept and blown all over
The sky. Perhaps two hearts, forlorn,
Yet mourn for him. Yet why? Why mourn?

The evening sky grew dark. The flowing
Stream's ripples hushed. A bug went buzz.

15. Gay country dances soon were going
To break. On river's bank there was
Sweet smoke from fishers' fires. There, strolling
By silv'ry moon, across the rolling
Green hillsides, sunk in deepest dream,
Alone, Tatyana crossed a stream.
She walked and walked. Then, unexpected,
She glimpsed a manor from her hill,
Some huts, a hillside grove, a rill
In which a garden was reflected.
She stared — and all at once her heart
Skipped sev'ral beats, and gave a start.

She feels a twinge of doubt and danger:
"What now — turn back, or go ahead?

16. He's far from home, and I'm a stranger...
Well, just the house and flower bed!"
And down the hill see Tanya dashing,
Quite out of breath and tensely flashing
Her glance about — confused, off guard...
She steps into an empty yard
And all at once, hounds charge her, barking.
Her shriek's so loud that servant boys
Appear from nowhere, making noise;
They calm the dogs (which can't help sparking
A tiff or two — a short-lived thing),
Then take their guest under their wing.

17. "The master's manor — might I see it?",
Tatyana asked, and right away
The boys ran off to fetch the key. It
Was next Anísya, old and gray,
Who trundled in with keys a-clinking.
The hall door soon swung wide, and slinking
Beneath our hero's noble crest,
Tatyana storms his empty nest.
She looks about; there, scratched and dusty,
Neglected, lies a billiard cue;
And there's a horsewhip, plain to view,
Upon a couch, old, patched and musty.
Tatyana hears Anísya drone:
"This hearth's where master sat alone.

18. And here with Lensky, our late neighbor,
He'd often sup, on winter eves.
Please come with me, dear. Here he'd labor,
Shuffling his papers by the sheaves.
Here quaffed he coffee; here slept oft he;
Here heard he briefings oh-so lofty,
And mornings, here he'd read a book.
His uncle, my old master, took
His naps here, too. It used to be that,
Sundays, by this window with me,
He'd deign to play at *durachkí.*•
God bless his loving soul, and see that
His bones in their damp grave know rest,
Nestled in Mother Earth's warm breast."

19. Tanya scans the room that surrounds her
With tender, loving, doe-like eyes.
It all seems priceless, and astounds her.
With heavy, heartsick soul she cries,
And reels from joys and pains united:
The table with its lamp, unlighted,
The pile of books, the cozy bed
Below the sill, the clean bedspread,
The modish portrait of Lord Byron,
The window's twilit moonlight scene,
An eerie glow, dim yet serene,
Napoleon's bustlet, cast in iron,
On a pedestal, frowning down,
Arms crossed tight, a hat for a crown.

20. A long time in the suave monk's cell bound,
She just stands fixed, though clock hands creep
And winds grow cold. The girl is spellbound;
She's gripped, transfixed. The grove's asleep
Of pines beside the foggy river,
And dark's the vale. Sky's silver sliver
Has slipped behind a craggy dome.
It's time our pilgrim headed home.
She tries to hide her agitation,
Yet can't suppress a sigh, but then
Tatyana's set to walk again.
She asks, though, first for dispensation
Once more to visit, on her own,
And scour his library, alone.

21. She bid adieu beyond the gateway
To old Anísya, then trudged back.
Next day at dawn, she rose and straightway
Set off along her prior track.
Once having gained his silent study,
She closed her eyes to everybody
And everything she knew outside.
Alone at last, she cried and cried.
Time passed, and soon she felt attracted
To all his books. And yet, at first
Their choice seemed strange. Her avid thirst
To read felt quenched. But then, distracted
By idle browsing, she got caught
In worlds whereof she'd never thought.

22. Although it had, we know, been ages
Since our Yevgeny'd sworn off books,
There nonetheless were certain pages
Exempted from his dirty looks:
Beside *Don Juan's* bard,* for example,
Stood sev'ral novels he'd still sample,
In which contemporary Man,
Our era, and its dreary plan,
Quite faithfully were represented,
Revealing Man's immoral soul,
How selfish he is, on the whole,
How dry, how dreamy, discontented;
Painting his spoiled and bitter brain,
Which roils and boils in pointless pain.

There could be found, on many pages,
The clenchmarks of his fingernails.
23. The girl, her gaze alert, engages
Two eager eyes upon these trails.
Tatyana notes, with trepidation,
The types of thought and observation
That struck Onegin forcefully —
Things he'd agreed with, silently.
The margins brought to her attention
Tracks from his pencil, trapped in coal.
Thus everywhere, Onegin's soul
Traduced itself, without intention:
Through jotted words, through checks and hooks,
Through interrogatory crooks.

And bit by bit, now she's progressing,
My Tanya starts to comprehend,
24. And e'er more clearly — there's a blessing! —
The man for whom her sighs won't end,
Thanks to her fate's imperious power —
This strange eccentric, fright'ning, sour,
This creature formed in heav'n or hell,
This angel, this smug ne'er-do-well.
What *is* he? Some cheap imitation?
A fatuous phantom? Or perchance
A Muscovite in Byron's stance?
Some copycat's interpretation,
Some bag of voguish phrase and gest —
Or worse, some parody, at best?

At last has she resolved the riddle,
Recalled the word that cuts the knot?
25. The hours had flown, little by little;
And lost in musings, she'd forgot
That back at home she was expected.
Her mother, there, in moans reflected:
"Tatyana's not a child. Oh, my!"
(This to some neighbors who'd dropped by.)
"Why, Olya's wed, yet Tanya's older...
I've got to find that girl a match —
It's time! But there's a fatal catch.
Her suitors get the coldest shoulder:
'No, thanks.' So mournful is her tone,
And through the woods she strays, alone."

26. "Mightn't she be in love?" "With whom, though?
Buyánov's ring was fast refused."
"And Petushkóv?" "Nice, but no groom, though.
Hussar Pykhtín was quite bemused
When to our home he came to visit;
He found Tatyana so exquisite
And fell so hard, my hopes were high —
But once again were dashed. Oh, why?"
"Come on, old gal, why are you waiting?
Try Moscow — heaven for a bride!
Why, beaus line up on every side!"
"Ach, friend, my income's been abating..."
"Enough for winter in your pot?
I'll gladly make a loan, if not."

27. Old Lárina was much agreed with
This sane suggestion, warm and kind;
And so she moved ahead full speed with
A Moscow winter's stay in mind.
Such plans caught Tanya unsuspecting.
She feared society's inspecting,
With rolling eyes, her simple traits,
Her country style, her hair in plaits,
Her dated clothes without pretension,
Her rural speech, so quaint and fey;
Sure, Moscow belles and blades would bray
With scorn, and snort in condescension.
Oh, terror! Safer far to stay
Ensconced in forests, far away.

28. Now with the sun's first rays arising,
Tatyana rushes to the leas,
And there, with fondest gaze apprising
Their flowing forms, she speaks with ease:
"Farewell, my valleys, soft and rolling,
And you, steep hills that I've known, strolling!
And you, familiar woodlands, aye!
Farewell, my lovely azure sky,
Farewell, o Nature, gay and gentle!
Your quiet world I soon shall trade
For glitter, noise, the vain parade...
Farewell, my freedom elemental!
What future am I heading for?
What secrets holds my fate in store?"

29. Her walks she's day by day extended.
Each time, some stream or hill or farm
Will stop her briefly with its splendid,
Though inadvertent, tranquil charm.
And as with friends one's known since nursing,
She sallies forth and starts conversing
With her old groves and friendly meads.
But summer far too swiftly speeds
And trees turn gold; fall's air is bracing.
Now Nature, trembling, short of breath,
Is all decked out for ritual death...
And here's the north, storm-clouds a-chasing,
Severely howling; now, no less,
Here's winter, chilly sorceress.

30. She came, she scattered, scintillated;
She drooped in clumps from old oak trees;
She left soft rugs that undulated
Across the hills and o'er the leas.
The river froze as sheets of shifting
White billows rose, all downy, drifting...
Glistens the frost, and we owe thanks
For Mother Winter's merry pranks.
But winter leaves Tatyana yawning;
Unlike the others, she feels gruff:
No wish to breathe in frosty fluff
Or rake fresh snow from outhouse awning
To wash her face or breast or arm;
This winter fills her with alarm.

31. The journey's start has long been sliding;
The final deadline's even passed.
But now a sleigh with brand-new siding,
Built for the ages, comes at last.
Its train is standard: three big wagons
Brimming with household stuff: glass flagons,
Porcelain bowls and chairs and trunks,
Mattresses, jams in jars, big bunks,
Feather-filled quilts, caged cocks, containers,
Pots, pans, rags — the list's not short —
Just goods, in sum, of every sort.
Then, in a hut, from sad retainers,
Loud sobs are heard — a parting din —
As eighteen steeds are ushered in.

32.

The nags are coupled to the coaches
While cooks whip up a hearty lunch.
The sleds are piled sky-high. Reproaches
Fly thick 'twixt coachmen and a bunch
Of sniffling serfs. A lean and scraggy
Old nag's now mounted by a shaggy
Young driver, while the servants crowd
The gate to wave and weep aloud.
The travelers take their seats, and slowly
The mighty coach slips out the gate.
"Farewell, my haunts, my calm estate!
Farewell, my shelters, lost and lowly!
Oh, will we meet again?" She cries,
And tears in streams flow from her eyes.

33.

When, to splendid illumination
Our state sweeps all its blocks away,
On that fine day (by calculation
Five centuries hence, our sages say),
Our ancient roads will serve us, surely,
Superbly, though they now serve poorly:
A network coursing here and there
Will crisscross Russia everywhere,
With chasms spanned by cast-iron bridges
Whose graceful arcs soar high and wide;
Sleek tunnels under bays will glide
In daring fashion; we'll cleave ridges
With classy pikes and, Christian-style,
With inns we'll bless them, one per mile.

34.

Our roads today are rotten, truly.
Forgotten bridges go to pot;
Our stopping-spots greet travelers cruelly,
With lots of fleas in every cot.
That's not enough? In chilly caverns
Hang frilly menus — shades of taverns! —
But just to tease the appetite.
Our blacksmiths are a further blight.
These rural Cyclops, as in fables,
Stand hunched o'er feebly-flick'ring flames
While fixing Europe's fancy frames
With Russian hammers banged on tables.
Our fatherland, meanwhile, they bless
For such a ditch-rich highway mess.

35. By contrast, when it's bleak and freezing,
To trek is pleasant, swift, and smooth.
Like jingles, flat and dull yet pleasing,
Hibernal trips can somehow soothe.
Our charioteers, they're deft and clever;
Our steeds, they tire out next to never.
Our verstposts charm the idle eye,
Like spaced-out fenceposts flashing by.•
The mistress, sad to say, had chosen,
From fear of highway robb'ry — tolls —
Not high-speed steeds, but home-grown foals.
Tatyana thus enjoyed the frozen
Barren and boring roadside sights
For sev'n full days and sev'n full nights.

36. But now they're drawing near the olden
White-stoned center of Moscow town,
Where many a cross, tall and golden,
Glints in the sunset like a crown.
O brothers! How my heart, it pounded,
When, all at once, I was surrounded
By churches, belfries with great bells,
Gardens, palaces, grand hotels!
How oft, in saddest separation,
Due to my wanderlusting fate,
I dreamt, o Moscow, of your gate!
"Moskvá"! Inside this appellation
The Russian heart hears noble sounds!
How much inside your name resounds!

37. Here, by its oakwood grounds surrounded,
Petrovsky Castle, in the gloom,
Ponders glories that late redounded
To it. Here, vainly, in some room,
Napoleon, drunk on recent vict'ry,
Awaited Moscow. Having tricked her, he
Quashed her, questing the Kremlin's keys.
But Moscow wouldn't soil her knees,
My Moscow, no — she'd not surrender.
Nor welcome gifts nor holidays
Did she prepare — instead, a blaze
To honor him who'd sought to rend her.
And from this room, sunk deep in thought,
He watched the flames and ruin they wrought.

38.
Farewell, o scene of prides departed,
Petrovsky Castle. Let's be fleet!
The rampart towers just now have started
To catch the light. Down Tversky Street
Careens our carriage o'er the cobbling,
While flashing by go ladies, squabbling,
Sentries and shoplets, sleds and scamps,
Gardens, cloisters, palaces, lamps,
Turks and troikas, chickens and pheasants,
Boulevards, towers, milliners, shacks,
Mounted Cossacks, elegant slacks,
Pushers of pills, old wobbling peasants,
Balconies, lions on gates, gold clocks,•
And, perched on crosses, jackdaw flocks.

[39]

40.
This final stretch — two hours of riding —
Left the voyagers tired and sore.
At last the coach stopped in a siding,
Chariton's Lane, before a door.
This was the house where, old and ailing,
Lived a dear aunt, her health now failing,
Racked by consumption four long years.
The door swings wide, and there appears
A graying Kalmuk, faithful servant
In glasses and a robe with rips.
With trembling hand, a sock he grips.
From the settee there comes a fervent
Shriek full of joy, and then takes place
A round of hugs, while greetings race:

41.
"*Princesse!*" "Pachette!" "Alína, dearie!"
"Who could've thought?" "Like long ago!"
"You're looking well." "And you're so cheery!"
"Sit down! I can't believe it, though —
I feel I'm in a fairy story!"
"Here's Tanya — she's my little glory."
"Tatyana, come! How young you seem!
Good grief, it's all so like a dream!
Dear cousin, say, do you remember
Your 'Grandison'?" "It rings a bell...
Ah, yes — of course! How's he? Do tell!"
"He came by carriage last December
From Simeon Street — a few blocks' ride.
He finally found his son a bride,

42. "But then... But let's save talk for later —
Why not, my darlings? Tanya's kin
She'll meet tomorrow. They await her,
And with such joy. But I'll stay in.
My legs are weak; too bad. How dreary!
Your travels must have left you weary;
Let's all lie down and take a rest...
Ach, I've no strength... My wilting breast...
For me, these days, just fun is dismal,
Let alone sadness... What a bore!
I'm good for nothing any more...
Old age, I tell you, is abysmal..."
Exhausted then, the aunt broke off,
Racked by tears and a raucous cough.

43. Sick Auntie's touch and gentle humor
Affect the girl, whose heart is soft;
She's ill at ease, though, as a roomer,
Used as she is to her old loft.
Shaded under a silken curtain,
She sleeps a sleep undeep, uncertain.
The early churchbells' booming sounds,
Which usher in the new morn's rounds,
Have dragged her from her bed, still groggy.
Awake, she sits upon the sill,
In hopes she'll glimpse a friendly hill,
As dawnlit, gloom becomes less foggy.
Instead, she sees strange fences, walls,
And courtyards, kitchens, horses' stalls.

44. And thus each day, to dull, protracted
Familial meals she's wheeled, to grin
And show her face, bored and distracted,
To grandmas, grandpas, sundry kin.
Far relatives from far-off places
Are bathed in kisses and embraces;
Fond exclamations flood her ears:
"How Tanya's grown! How many years
Since you were christened! How time's speeding!"
"How long, dear, since you graced my lap!"
"And since I gave your ears a slap!"
"My ginger snaps capped off each feeding!"
And with one voice, the grannies groan,
"How fast, alas, our years have flown!"

Chapter VII

45. Their changes, though, are few and scanty.
They all seem rut-stuck, bound by rule:
Princess Eléna, wealthy auntie,
Sports that same old bonnet of tulle;
Still dreams up schemes Lyubóv Petróvna;
Still gleams from creams Lukérya Lvóvna;
Iván Petróvich? Not yet bright.
Semyón Petróvich? Wad's yet tight.
Aunt Pelagéya, as expected,
Brought her companion, Herr Kleinmaus, •
Her same old spitz, her same old spouse,
Who's still a club-man most respected,
Meek and deaf as he used to be,
Gobbling and guzzling, though, for three. •

46. The younger girls hug Tanya warily.
These Moscow graces, once let go,
Discreetly scan and sniff her, verily
Checking her out from head to toe.
At first they find her quite exotic:
Provincial and a bit neurotic,
Too pale, for sure, and slightly thin,
But then again, not ugly as sin —
And soon, in line with laws of passion,
They melt and merge her to their band,
They kiss and warmly press her hand,
They fluff her curls in current fashion,
And in their singsong girlish styles
Confide their secret wiles and guiles,

47. Their own as well as girlfriends' catches,
Their hopes and pranks and dreams and trysts.
Their frilly banter's offhand snatches
Are spiced with slightly acid twists.
Then, in exchange for all this oily
Palaver, they start asking coyly
That Tanya too should bare her breast,
But Tanya's somehow not impressed.
She hears their words as if in rêv'rie:
She fathoms none, nor cares at all.
As for her own heart's strongest call —
Her joys, her fears — she holds back ev'ry
External trace, maintains her grace,
Lest someone peer behind her face.

48.
How Tanya'd relish taking part in
Their larger and their smaller talk!
But in the parlor, there's no art in
The parley; it's just frothy squawk.
In wit, they range from bland to blander;
They're boring even when they slander.
In all their sterile, arid speech,
Their news and gossip, points they preach,
For days on end, no flash comes poking
Out of the ashen coals, by chance
Or luck. These spirits cannot dance.
Their hearts beat slow, even when joking.
How sad, thou empty upper crust:
Your best buffoon is but a bust.

49.
Tatyana's keenly watched by strutting
Youths in cushy government jobs,•
Who've aught to do, aside from cutting
Her down, these princely simpering snobs.
One fool among them, quite pathetic,
Finds her ideally sympathetic,
And while he leans against a door,
Pens an elegy she'll ignore.
Friend Vyázemsky• once sat beside her
At sick old Aunt's; his sparkling wit
Tickled her fancy for a bit.
Meanwhile, some sycophant's espied her;
He asks about her, does this prig,
While fiddling with his powdered wig.

50.
Where Muse Melpómene's• sad wailing
Resounds forever, like a storm,
And where, her tinsel banner flailing,
For frigid crowds she must perform;
Where Muse Thalía gently dozes
Despite her clamoring public's roses;
And where some youth who's in a trance
Loves only Muse Terpsíchore's dance
(When we were youths, mere lads and lasses,
'Twas much the same, and thus it's stayed),
There turn no eyes toward our maid:
Not ladies' jealous opera glasses,
Nor those of gents who put on airs,
Who sit in stalls or velvet chairs.

51.
To the Sobránie* she's escorted
(The nobles' ballroom), where the crush,
The heat and tumult and distorted
Old airs, the couples' whirling rush,
The belles' fine gowns, the candles' brightness,
The grand bouquets, the hubbub's tightness,
The nubile damsels in a clutch,
Assault one's senses overmuch.
Here boulevardiers of notoriety
Show off their vests and derring-do,
And show, offhand, their lorgnettes, too.
Here cuirassiers meet high society:
On leave, they thunder in, flash spurs
And sunder hearts, depart in blurs.

52.
At night the lovely stars are many;
Of lovelies Moscow's got its share.
For brightness, though, night hasn't any
To match the moon, blue air's queen fair.
But she whose beauty makes me cower
Transcends, alas, my lyre's power.
So like the moon, grand on its throne,
'Mongst dames and maids she shines alone.
In proud, serene, celestial dances,
Above the earth she softly glides,
And in her breast what bliss resides!
What mystery in her mooning glances!
But stop; it's time you drew the line,
For now you've knelt at folly's shrine.

53.
The din, the cackling, bows and flitting,
Galop, mazurka, waltz... And there's
Tatyana. Flanked by aunts, she's sitting
Beside a column — no one cares.
She stares and stares, yet always blankly;
She hates this grand world's tumult, frankly.
It's stifling here... and, in a dream,
She sails away to field and stream,
Back to the backwoods' humble peasants,
Back to that lonely, tranquil nook
Where, bubbling, flows her lively brook;
Back to her books, her private pleasance,
The shadows in the linden lane,
The spot where *he'd* appeared, her swain.

And thus in thoughts, far off she's flying,
Leaving the frenzied crowd and ball;
54. Meanwhile, some lofty general's eyeing
Our girl, who's got him in her thrall.
Her aunties watch each other, nodding;
Then, with their elbows, both make prodding
Pokes in her ribs, and softly say:
"Look to your left, niece — right away."
"Look to my left? But where? And wherefore?"
"Don't ask — just use your eyes and hunt!
See, in that group up near the front,
Two in uniform? They've been there for...
Oh — he just rose — just spun about..."
"That general? Him?! The one that's stout?"

Here I shall let her bask in glory,
Sweet Tanya dear, to whom I cling,
55. For here we briefly shelve our story,
Lest we lose track of whom I sing —
On whom three words now (plus three dozen):•
I praise a youthful friend and cousin,
I sing his life, full many a quirk,
And pray that to my drawn-out work,
You'll render, epic muse, your blessing.
A trusty staff you've tendered me;
May I not blunder aimlessly.
Enough; no longer's duty pressing!
To classic style I've tipped my hat.
Though late, my foreword's done; that's that!•

Chapter Eight

Fare thee well, and if for ever,
Still for ever, fare thee well.
— Byron[•]

1.
Those early days, when I was blooming,
Budding serenely *au Lycée,*[•]
Apuleius seemed all-consuming,
While Cicero's thoughts drove mine astray;
Those early days, in mystic valleys
In spring, where water whirls and dallies
In quiet creeks, and swans are heard,
My muse's visits first occurred,
And all at once my monkish dwelling
Was filled with light; my muse revealed
A pot-pourri ere then concealed
Of art's new ploys, in ballads telling
Of children's joys, of our grand past,
And dreams that make slow heartbeats fast.

2.
The world I swirled in met her smiling,
And on her wings I met success:
Near death, Derzhávin[•] deemed beguiling
My fledgling verselets *sans finesse.*
"And Dmítriev, too, endured my lays" (Pope);[•]
While Karamzín,[•] for Russia, raised hope:
He shucked old shackles, stroked the muse,
And saved us, through reformist views.
Zhukóvsky[•] — *et tu,* Beauty's champion,
Inspired by all that's deep, thou art,
Thou idol of each virgin heart —
Was it not thou who, with thy lampion,
Showed me the way and urged I chart,
Toward worldly fame, a path apart?

And so, as my sole law declaring
The tyranny of passions' sway,
3.   And too, the crowd's deep feelings sharing,
I spirited my muse away
To feasts uproarious and fight-full
(To night patrollers, weird and frightful);
And, in return, to these gay whirls
She brought her gifts of verbal pearls
And frisked just like a bacchanalian;
To earn a cup she sang some rhymes,
And all those youths of bygone times
Pursued with glee my madcap alien;
And 'mongst my friends I swelled with pride
That this free spirit graced my side.

But soon their circle I abandoned
For distant climes... and she with me.
4.   How oft, when trav'ling over land and
On waterways, the silence she
Would break, with magic, secret tales!
How oft, on high Caucasian trails
Up moonlit slopes, she, like Lenore,•
Would share my steed and race, full-bore!
How oft, upon the banks of Tauris,•
She led me through nocturnal mist
To hear the sea that howled and hissed —
The Nereids'• incessant chorus,
The billows' deep and timeless hymn
To him who hewed the cosmic rim.

Our capital but scarce recalling —
Its glitter, its loud merriments —
5.   In sad Moldavia's deserts sprawling
She visited the humble tents
Of nomad tribes, and there this child
Of cultured ways turned strange and wild.
She lost the limpid words divine
She'd known, and learned new tongues less fine
And songs from distant steppes endearing...
But all at once her whole world flipped:
Now in my garden, lo, she's slipped,
And as a country maid's appearing —
A pensive lass of downcast look,
Who holds some French romantic book.

6.

And now, for novelty, I'm carting
My muse to some high-class *soirée*;
To eye her steppe-tinged charms I'm darting
My jealous, timid glance her way —
Which now she threads through diplomatic
Careerists, and aristocratic
Bluebloods, *grandes dames,* and army fops;
And then in perfect calm she stops
To sit and scan, with admiration,
The hostess with her mingling guests,
Tight crush, fine clothes, glib gab, grand gestes...
She notes, as 'round an illustration,
Around each debutante and dame,
A clump of tall, dark men: a frame.

7.

She loves the harmony and order
Upon this oligarchic stage;
Even the condescension toward her,
The random mix of rank and age...
But in this chosen crowd, there, wistful,
Who's standing wordless, eyes all mistful?
His face, to all, looks strange and grim;
Their blurry faces look, to him,
Just like a row of spooks bored dizzy.
And is it prideful hurt, or spleen,
That permeates his mournful mien?
How come Onegin's here — or is he?
Who else? 'Tis no one else. "So then
He's back amongst us — but since when?"

8.

Has he stayed fixed, or grown more mellow?
Does still he act the oddball's part?
Pray tell, this new Eugene's which fellow?
With what new role will now he start?
What face will he put on, the faker —
That of a bigot, or a Quaker,
A patriot, or cosmopolite?
Harold? Melmoth? Or else just might
He don the mask no one supposes —
The "good boy" mask, like yours and mine?
Were I in *his* shoes, I'd incline
To leave behind outmoded poses.
He's gulled the world too long, and so...
"You *know* him?" Know him? Yes and no.

"Oh, tell me, then: Wherefore the grudging
Objections, when you speak of him?

9.   Only because we're always judging
Or fussing over every whim?
Or that a fiery spirit's rashness
Offends small souls that lack in brashness
Or spurs the smug to snort, 'Ho ho'?
Or that a nitwit's mind can't grow?
Or that we take some sweet-talk's contents
On credit, as if words were deeds?
Or that to malice folly leads?
Or that puffed egos love puffed nonsense?
Or that true mediocrity's
Our sugar pill, not our disease?"

But blest is he who's sidestepped oldness;
Blest he who grew up not too fast;

10.   Who slowly learned to stand life's coldness
As summers, springs, falls, winters passed;
Who's ne'er been prone to dreams of yearning,
Who ne'er the social whirl went spurning;
Who was, at twenty, blade or swell,
But ten years later, married well;
Who, fifty now, has no outstanding
Personal debts, or other types;
Who earned his glory, wealth, and stripes
Serenely, though with girth expanding;
Of whom 'tis whispered all the time:
"Old So-and-So? A chap sublime!"

How sad it is, to think youth's flower
In vain was given us; that we

11.   Betrayed her with each passing hour
While she deceived us equally;
That all our fondest aspirations
And dreams were but hallucinations
That one by one went down the drain,
Like rotting leaves in autumn rain.
It's grim to see before you looming
The same old meal night after night,
To see life as one solemn rite,
To imitate the crowd's fine grooming,
Its high-class act, while sharing naught
With it, in fact, in aim or thought.

The subject of harsh scrutinizing
Will find it grim (you must agree)
12. To learn that thoughtful gentry's sizing
Him up, and in him tends to see
A sad-faced crank, a misfit phony,
If not some monstrous Satan-crony —
Or worse: my Demon,• raging doubt.
Eugene (it's time to trot him out)
Had slain his comrade in a duel
And reached the age of twenty-six
Without a goal on which to fix
His sights — a victim of the cruel
Disease of apathy, his life
Adrift: no work, no wish, no wife.

Consumed was he by consternation:
The sense he ought to shift his lair
13. (A most unpleasant situation,
A cross that few would gladly bear).
He left his country habitation,
The fields' and forests' isolation,
Where visions of a bloodied shade
Upon him daily darkly weighed,
And roamed, deprived of destination,
With but one hope inside his head;
Yet all his trav'ling only led,
As do all things, to aggravation;
Like Chatsky *de retour* from France,
He found he'd hopped from deck to dance.•

Across the crowd excitement rippled,
Across the ballroom whispers sped,
14. As toward the hostess marched a crippled
And princely general, while ahead
Sashayed a lady, calm and gracious.
She wasn't haughty or loquacious,
She had no arrogance of gaze,
She spoke not one pretentious phrase,
She showed no facial affectation,
She made no imitative ploys;
She was a paragon of poise,
And seemed the perfect incarnation —
(All my regrets, Shishkóv;• I know
Anglais it's not) — of *comme il faut*.

15.
The ladies toward her were advancing;
The old ones smiled as she passed by;
The gentlemen found her entrancing,
And deeply bowed to catch her eye;
The younger girls went walking by her
More quietly; but holding higher
His head and shoulders than the crowd,
Her general strode, aloof and proud.
No one could honestly have called her
A beauty, but from head to toe,
Nowhere could critics find or show
That which in certain of the balder
Of London's upper classes, they
Deem "vulgar". (Oh, that word... I say!

16.
I love the word, but can't translate it.
With us, it's relatively new;
Some like it, but some others hate it —
It's held in high esteem by few;
In epigrams, it might be splendid...)•
But ho! Milady's tale's not ended.
With carefree charm she sweetly sat
By Nina Voronskáya,• that
Bedazzling Cleopatra double
Who hails from our fair Neva's banks;
On one thing, you and I'd close ranks:
That Nina's table-mate spelled trouble,
For Nina's gleaming marble face
Could not eclipse her neighbor's grace.

17.
"I wonder...", meditates Yevgeny,
"Could that be... Well, of course! And yet...
From deepest steppes? No, it's too zany..."
He keeps his obstinate lorgnette
Upon a certain face directed —
The one that's made him feel connected
Anew with features long forgot.
"You'd know her, surely, would you not,
Prince — with the Spanish delegation
She's chatting, in a crimson cap."
The prince stares back, and cries, "Dear chap,
You're really out of circulation!
I'd like you two to meet, so come!"
"But tell me who..." "My wife, old chum."

18. "I hadn't heard. How nice you've brought her!
You married when?" "Two years ago."
"And who's the girl?" "The Larins' daughter."
"Tatyana?" "That's the one. You know
Each other, then?" "Our land's adjacent."
"Well, well — small world!" The prince, complacent,
Goes up to greet his wife, and brings
His kin and friend of many springs.
She might have hit her soul's dark nadir
When she, as princess, looked at him,
But stunned or struck, or grave or grim,
She gave no signal that betrayed her;
Instead, she kept her perfect poise
And bowed without the slightest noise.

19. Indeed, she wasn't just untrembling,
But never even shifted shade;
Her brow ne'er twitched... Was she dissembling?
Who knows? Her mouth seemed unafraid.
Onegin watched her, but no matter
How keen his gaze, could not get at her
Familiar core — gone with the wind...
His wordlessness left him chagrined,
But words just failed him. She, though, queried
How long he'd been there, whence he'd come,
How fared his farm... Small talk, in sum.
And then she flashed her spouse a wearied
Expression, so they sauntered from
The room, to leave him dazed and numb.

20. Was this the selfsame trembling frail
Young girl to whom he once, alone,
In the beginning of our tale,
In deep, dark, far-off lands unknown,
In a grand blaze of moralizing,
Had spoken sternly, sermonizing?
Was this the selfsame maid from whom
He'd kept a letter in his room,
Where spoke the heart, without restriction?
Was this the girl... or did he dream?...
Was this the girl whose self-esteem
He'd crushed, despite her sad affliction?
Could *she* just now have been, in truth,
So cool to him, and so uncouth?

21. He leaves the packed *soirée,* and, pensive,
Goes home to get a good night's rest,
But in his sleep grows apprehensive,
Disturbed by dreams, some damned, some blessed.
He wakes despite not having rested;
A note is brought. Prince N's• requested
The pleasure of his company...
"Tonight? Good grief! I'll go! It's she!"
A suave response he scribbles quickly.
But what's got into him? Strange dreams!
There's something shifting at the seams
That bind his soul, so cold and sickly —
But what? Vexation? Vanity?
Or else, once more, young love's ennui?

22. Once more, the hours Eugene is counting;
Once more, day's end he can't await.
Strikes ten at last. With pressures mounting,
He flies, he flees, he's at the gate,
He walks straight in, his heart a-flutter.
The princess sits, he sees, in utter
Aloneness, so he joins her there,
And there they sit, but talk is spare:
Long, awkward silences afflict him.
Thoughts bubble up from mem'ry's bank,
Yet when she speaks, his mind goes blank:
Once more, he's wordlessness's victim.
He stares at her in turmoil; she,
By contrast, sits relaxed and free.

23. Her husband's coming puts a halt to
This quite unpleasant *tête-à-tête;*
Eugene and he recall their all-too
Few antic antics, when they'd met.
While these two laugh, guests fill the palace,
And with the salt of worldly malice
The conversation comes alive.
Before the hostess, facile jive
Flashed swiftly with no affectation,
And with it mingled nonsense-free
Straight talk that lacked all pedantry
Or cheapness or pontification —
Straight talk so open, bright, and clear
It didn't shock a single ear.

Chapter VIII

24.

The blooms of Petersburg society,
The upper sets, the fashion plates,
The standard faces — no variety —
And fools well-schooled in crashing gates
Were here, quite near some dames quite hoary
In caps and nosegays — all quite gory;
Here, too, was found a flock of maids
Whose visages wore somber shades,
And then, of course, the envoy going
Great guns on some grim state affair,
And, too, with scented, graying hair,
An oldster, constantly *bon-mot*'ing
In olden style, and with such flair
That these days, sadly, it seems square.

25.

The hostess' tea is far too cloying —
So thought an epigrammist gent
Who found most everything annoying —
The men's drab tone, the dames' bland bent,
Dull chat on novels sentimental,
Two sisters' bangles ornamental,
The lying press, how war twists life,
The snow, and even his young wife.
[These last six lines are oft omitted,
And therefore, by a fluke of fate,
Your translator can speculate...
One hardly needs to be quick-witted
To wonder if our author meant
To hint that he himself's that "gent"...]

26.

Prolásov• brought his reputation,
Well-earned, for boorishness along;
Through withering impersonation,
Saint-Priest,• in albums for the throng,
You penciled him to death, in your way.
Meanwhile there posed, just by the doorway,
Cherubic, picture-prim, and hushed,
Some ballroom clotheshorse, laced and flushed;
And then arrived a stray wayfarer,
A scoundrel in a too-starched vest,
Who entertained more than one guest
By feigning that he felt no terror;
A verdict came down from the crowd
Through silent glances, not aloud.

Chapter VIII   ➤➤ 127

27.
As for Eugene, there was for him mid
The whole assembly but one face:
Not of that girl once pale, once timid,
Once simple, trapped in love's vain chase,
But of this princess so uncaring,
This goddess with her frigid bearing —
She of the queenly, grand Nevá.
Oh, mortals! To your Ur-mamá
Old Eve, you owe your fatal features!
With what you've got, too soon you're bored;
And to the tree banned by the Lord
The snake e'er lures you wanton creatures;
God's paradise for you is moot,
Unless it yields forbidden fruit.

28.
Tatyana's certainly swapped banners!
How snugly in this role she fits!
How swiftly she took on the manners
That one must don when high one sits!
Who'd dare to seek that maiden tender
In this majestic, carefree lender
Of laws to some grand ballroom fest?
To think that once he'd stirred her breast!
To think she'd lain for hours, anguished,
Ere Morpheus would still her cries,
And sighed for him her virgin sighs,
And moonward lifted eyes that languished
To dream a dream that some fine day
Down humble paths, as one, they'd stray!

29.
Each age respects love in its fashion;
But hearts that just have taken wing
Derive much good from surging passion,
As meadows from cloudbursts in spring:
They freshen in the rains of yearning,
Renew themselves, while riper turning;
Thus rendered potent, life takes root
And bursts with bloom and luscious fruit.
But once we're old and turning sterile,
Once past the cusp of life's best years,
Love's trace will die, to leave but tears...
Thus chilly fall puts meads in peril,
For in its storms they turn to bogs,
And trees to skeletons and logs.

No doubt! Alas, Eugene is swooning —
In love with Tanya, like a child.

30. In anguish and in lovelorn mooning
He spends each night and day, beguiled.
Ignoring all his mind's reproaches,
In coach he every day approaches
Her porch and glassed-in entrance hall,
And stalks her, shadowlike, in thrall.
He's happy if he gets to wrap her
Sweet shoulders in a swirl of fur,
Or if, by chance, he touches her,
Or if he splits her train of dapper
And oh-so lucky lackeys, or
Can pluck her kerchief from the floor.

But does she notice? Tanya doesn't —
No matter how he twists and turns —

31. As if a friend Onegin wasn't.
She alternately greets and spurns
Eugene, now giving him a curtsey,
Now acting curt — but does she flirt? She
Refrains; for she's not got one drop
Of flirting blood; they'd make her stop
In her high world, were she found flirting.
Onegin's turning pale; but she
Seems not to care, or not to see.
Perhaps consumption's why he's hurting?
He's sent to doctors for his blahs;
The latter send him to the spas.

But spa-trips he declines; he'd rather
Announce by post that soon he'll clench

32. His father and his father's father —
But she's unmoved (like any wench).
Still, he persists, there's no denying;
He keeps on hoping, keeps on trying.
Although he's sick and weak, he's bold,
And bravely wills that truth be told:
He pens to her an ardent letter.
How come? He's always rightly thought
That letter-writing's good for naught!
Well, pain has finally got the better
Of him; pain's made his vision blurred.
So here's his letter, word for word.

You'll be offended, I foresee,
By my sad secret's revelation,
Your haughty look the incarnation
Of bitterness and scorn for me.
What might I seek, and with what reason
Unveil the hopes that cloud my brow?
In you, what smirks of spiteful treason
Will I perchance give rise to now?

When first we met, in random fashion,
I sensed a spark in your compassion,
Yet in it scarcely dared to trust:
Sweet vice I would not let get started;
From freedom I would loath be parted —
My loathsome freedom, now worth dust.
By one more blow were then we riven...
In sacrifice poor Lensky fell,
And from that moment, I felt driven
To bring about my heart's death-knell.
A friend to none, from friendship buffered,
My God! with freedom drunk, this boy
Thought calm a substitute for joy.
How wrong he was, and how he's suffered!

Instead, to watch you all the time,
And in your wake to follow, raving;
To catch your smile, your glance sublime,
In mine, so blinded by my craving;
To hear you speak, and with my soul
Your deep divinity to capture;
Before your eyes to drown in dole,
To faint, to pale, to perish... Rapture!

But I'm deprived of this; for you,
I run around all helter-skelter;
Each day is dear; each hour, too;
Yet I in pointless boredom welter
And waste my fate-allotted days.
Oh, how each one upon me weighs!
I've little time, I know, remaining,
Yet if each morning I were sure
That all day long o'er me were reigning
Your grace, my life would long endure...

I fear that in this humble prayer
You'll think you see — from far, aloof —
A cunning ploy your soul to snare;
I nearly hear your stern reproof.

Chapter VIII

If you but knew how deep the aching
When love makes one fair burn with thirst —
When reason's all one has, for slaking
The fire that makes one's veins fair burst!
Were I with you, I'd sink, embracing
Your knees, and then in tears I'd pour
My heart out in lament, retracing
My sins, my hopes, and much, much more.
But for the nonce, with feigned composure,
I offer you a merry smile,
I keep my words and eyes in file,
And give my feelings scant exposure!

Yet such is life; the needed grit
To fight myself exceeds my measure.
Les jeux sont faits; it's now your pleasure
To deal with me as you see fit.

33.
No answer. To a second missive
And then a third, no word's returned.
What's wrong? How come she's so dismissive?
No answer... Why so unconcerned?
An evening ball... She coolly greets him,
But then ignores him and mistreats him.
My God! Those once-warm eyes exude
A harsh and wintry Twelfthtide mood!
A with'ring sneer, all cold and ashen,
She scarce can manage to contain.
Onegin stares and stares in vain:
Where went her turmoil, her compassion?
Where went her tear-stains? Down the drain!
Her face spells rage; her warmth's been slain.

34.
Mightn't her visage hint she's fearful
Her husband or their set could sense
The deeper meaning of some cheerful
Remarks or friendly "accidents",
And guess therefrom the link they're sharing?...
O, hopeless hope! He leaves, despairing,
Cursing his curséd craziness;
Then, drowning in its curséd mess,
He shuns all contact with society
While in his study's silent gloom,
Before him, bitter memories loom:
A hubbub... Chased by deep anxiety,
He's caught, he's collared, and he's blocked,
And in some far dark corner locked.

35.
He reads without discrimination:
Manzoni, Fontenelle, Chamfort,*
And Gibbon — books from every nation —
Rousseau and Herder — these and more —
Madame de Staël and Bayle the skeptic,
Tissot, Bichat — he's so eclectic!
He reads a bit of Russian stuff
But never thinks he's read enough —
In highbrow almanacs and journals
Where sermons far too oft are heard,
And where your author's oft been slurred —
Yet now and then I've savored kernels
Of truth in madrigals, not slurs:
È sempre bene,* my good sirs.

36.
His eyes were reading, but... what of it?
To distant climes his thoughts all stole.
His tears, his dreams, all he might covet,
Kept swarming deeply in his soul.
Across each page his eyes went speeding,
But 'tween the lines, his mind was reading
Quite other lines, and in them he
Was drowning irretrievably.
From all these lines sprang strange upwellings:
Dark legends from the secret past
And dreams detached from every last
Familiar face; and threats, foretellings,
The zany plot of some long tale —
Or missives from a maiden frail.

37.
And bit by bit, in thought and feeling
He sinks toward numbness, drab and bland;
Meanwhile, his fantasy starts dealing
Before his eyes a motley hand:
Sometimes he'll see, where snows are thawing,
A youth lies, placid, barely drawing
A breath, as if asleep in bed;
Eugene hears voices: "What?" "He's dead."
Sometimes he'll see old foes, forgotten,
And slanderers, and pluckless cads,
A swarm of maids who've dumped their lads,
Some band of cronies, base and rotten...
Sometimes a country manse he'll see,
Where sillside sitting, still there's *she*...

38. So oft he daydreamed, tossed by passion,
He very nearly lost his mind
And turned a bard in his own fashion —
Yet truth to tell, he would have shined!
By virtue of its lure hypnotic,
He nearly grasped our patriotic
Poetic science's deep laws,
My pupil plagued by metric flaws.
The poet's role seemed most becoming
To him when in some nook he'd hide
Alone before a fireside,
And — *Benedetta* idly humming,
Or *Idol Mio** — lost in haze,
Tossed book or slipper on the blaze.

39. The air grew warm as days went flying,
And winter knew to call it quits.
Eugene gave up his versifying,
But not the ghost, and not his wits.
He's lent new life by buds aborning,
And first thing on some clear spring morning
He leaves his cloistered, small *château*
Where, marmot-like, he'd braved the snow.
He shuts his windows, sweeps his ingle,
And skirts the Neva in his sleigh,
Where sunbeams on blue iceblocks play.
Below him, rutted snowdrifts mingle
With mud, and quickly turn to slush.
But whither, thereupon, does rush

40. Onegin? In anticipation,
You've guessed it right (an easy trick):
Tatyana's was the destination
Of my persistent maverick.
He enters, a cadaver seeming,
Through empty entrance-way goes streaming,
Then hall, then further — still no face.
He cracks a door, and has to brace
Himself — but why? What's so distressing?
The princess sits before him, frail,
Disheveled, in her robe, all pale;
Her cheek against one hand is pressing.
She holds some note and, as she reads,
The tears flow down like tiny beads.

'Twas but a glimpse, yet who could fail
To spot her suff'ring's muffled trace?
41. Behind this princess's cool veil,
Who'd not have known poor Tanya's face?
Eugene fell down before her, kneeling,
From both regret and pity reeling;
She shuddered; then with wordless eyes
Regarded him without surprise
Or anger; and his languor-laden
And feeble gaze, his pleading look
And mute reproach, were like a book
To her: so clear! That simple maiden
Who once was dreamy, once was warm,
Now's resurrected in new form.

She lets him kneel, so low, so needy,
But keeps her eyes upon him, and
42. Allows his lips athirst and greedy
To rest against her senseless hand.
What thoughts could lie behind her action?
The silence lingered in protraction,
But then, at last, came her soft voice:
"Enough; arise. I'm left no choice:
I'll bare my soul, and not obliquely.
Onegin, do you still recall
When on the garden path, one fall,
Fate had us meet, and there, I meekly
Heard out your preaching till the end?
Well, now the worm has turned, my friend.

"Onegin, those days I was younger
And looked it, too — yes, I'm resigned;
43. For you I felt such gnawing hunger,
Yet in your heart, what did I find?
What kind of answer? Harshness only —
Or am I wrong? To you, some lonely
Young maiden's love was hardly new —
But now, my blood chills through and through
Each time I recollect your preaching
And see that frosty look again...
But I don't blame you; no, back then,
You spurned most nobly my beseeching.
My God! How fair you were with me,
And e'er my soul shall grateful be...

Chapter VIII

44. "Back then — and if I'm wrong, correct me —
In quiet woods, far from this crush,
You found it easy to reject me;
So what's behind love's sudden rush?
How come I'm now your life's sole focus?
Perhaps the flashy hocus-pocus
Of my new clique exudes panache?
Or is it my cachet and cash?
Or is it that the courtlings court us
Because my man in war was maimed?
Or is it that, should we be shamed
And should the haughty court then snort us
Into the gutter, you would smell
The smell of roses, as we fell?

45. "This makes me weep... If you recall your
Young Tanya as she was of old,
Then know: the searing sting of all your
Rebukes that day, so stern, so cold,
I'd sooner suffer, any hour —
If only it were in my power —
Than all your sniveling notes and tears.
At least my youthful hopes and fears
Once woke in you some trace of feeling:
You showed respect for my few years...
But now? My spurner reappears
And casts himself before me, kneeling?
Don't make me laugh, you who behave
Like pettiness's simpering slave!

46. "Alas, Onegin, all these splendors,
The frills that drape my dreary days,
My triumphs 'midst these court pretenders,
My modish home, my grand *soirées,*
I'd give up in a flash. What matters
Is not our masquerades' cheap tatters,
And all their smoke and shine and squawks;
What matters is those garden walks,
My books, our manse so ordinary:
Those places where, long long ago,
Onegin, first I came to know
Your face; and yes, that cemetery
Where now a cross and treelimbs' shade
Keep watch where my poor nanny's laid...

47.
"Back then, to us, bliss all but beckoned;
We came so close!... But now my fate
Is cast in stone. Perhaps I reckoned
Too rashly when I closed the gate,
But mother, weeping, kept imploring,
And since no path appeared less boring
Than any other path to poor
Tatyana, I just settled for
A mate. And now you must be leaving,
I beg you. Yes, I know, inside
Your heart live honor, strength, and pride;
And yes, I love you still (deceiving
Is pointless now); but since I'm wed,
I'll keep my vows until I'm dead."

48.
And out she strode. Eugene stands shattered
As if by thunder's awesome blast.
His breast's awash with grief; he's battered,
Adrift in raging seas, aghast.
But hark — some spurs are heard, encroaching;
It's Tanya's husband, fast approaching...
And at this juncture grave and grim
We'll let my hero sink or swim,
O reader dear; we'll take vacations
From him, for now, forevermore.
It's been enough! We've come ashore
At last, we two! Congratulations
Upon our finally reaching port.
Hurrah! What's left is sweet and short.

49.
Dear reader, friend or foe, at present
I'd like — whoever you might be —
To take my leave on terms most pleasant.
And thus farewell. Whate'er from me
You sought in this or that light stanza —
Some boist'rous souvenir bonanza,
Relief from toils and drudgery,
Some lively scenes, some *jeux d'esprit* —
Perhaps just errors in my grammar! —
God grant that in my modest art,
For entertainment, for your heart,
For dreams, or for the press's yammer,
You've found at least a grain or two.
And on that note, farewell to you!

50. Farewell to you, Eugene, queer cohort,
And you, my feminine ideal,
And you, my book, for though you're *so* short,
You're faithful, and you've such appeal.
Together, you've provided for me
A haven from my life so stormy,
Sweet talk with friends: a poet's yen.
It seems a life's flashed by since when
My young and fresh Tatyana and her
Sad friend Onegin, in my dreams,
First came to me as vague, dim gleams;
Just how my novel might meander
Back then I couldn't yet infer:
My magic crystal showed but blur.

51. But of that crew to whom, as brothers,
So proudly my first lines I read,
A few no longer live, while others
Are distant, as once Saadi said.•
Eugene's been sketched without their knowing.
And as for her whose lifeblood's flowing
Through Tanya's portrait's every touch...
Oh, Fate has fled with far too much!
Blest he who quit life's celebration
Ne'er having seen its full design,
Nor having drained his cup of wine;
Who shelved the book of life's narration
Before he'd read its final line,
As I now, with Onegin mine.

Notes

A Note on the Notes

*I am not nearly as much of a literary scholar as
you might tend to infer from perusing the following
notes. I am, however, perfectly capable of using an
encyclopedia, of reading other people's notes, and of
paraphrasing. So there you have it.*   *— DRH.*

p. xli   *Pétri de vanité...*: "Bloated with vanity, he had even
more of that brand of pride that makes its owner lay
claim to good and bad deeds with equal indifference,
thanks to a perhaps-mistaken sense of superiority."
(From a private letter, probably written by Pushkin.)

"   *Not aiming to amuse... distilled from tears*: Pushkin's novel
in verse was originally dedicated to Pyotr Alexeevich
Pletnyov, its first publisher and a friend of the author's.
In later editions, though, Pletnyov's name was removed
from the page, leaving the poem to stand alone.

Chapter I

epigraph   *Prince Vyázemsky*: This is Pyotr Andreevich Vyazemsky
(1792–1878) — a critic, wag, romantic poet, and close
friend of Pushkin's. Here, in his poem *First Snow*,
Vyazemsky likens the passing of youth to a sleigh ride.

I.1   *My uncle, matchless moral model*: The novel's opening
line (literally "My uncle, of most honest principles")
imitates the opening line of a fable by Ivan Krylov
(1796–1844): "An ass of most honest principles".

I.2   *Ruslán and Lyudmíla*: An earlier work by Pushkin — a
fairy tale in verse — which launched his reputation as a
writer.

"   *The North was, shall I say, "severe"*: "Written in
Bessarabia" (Pushkin's note). With this line, Pushkin is
alluding to his exile (which lasted from 1820 to 1826)
from Saint Petersburg to parts south, for having written
some slightly subversive verses.

I.3   *Letny Park*: Or the Summer Garden — a Petersburg
park on the banks of the Neva.

I.6   *Juvenal*: Decimus Junius Juvenalis, a Roman satirical
poet (ca. 55–140), often read by students of Latin.

I.7   *Theocritus*: Greek poet (ca. 310–250 B.C.), famous for
his bucolic idylls.

I.8   *Naso*: Publius Ovidius Naso, elegiac and erotic Roman
poet (43 B.C.–17 A.D.), most famous for his *Art of Love*

and for his fifteen-volume poetic work *Metamorphoses*. Exiled for alleged immoral acts, he died in Moldavia.

I.9   (Missing stanza I.9): There are numerous stanzas of *Eugene Onegin* that Pushkin deleted for various reasons, including anticipated censorship. These are indicated, as here, by numerals in brackets.

I.12   *Faublas*: The hero of a picaresque novel by Louvet de Couvrai (1760–1797); Faublas is an infamous seducer of other men's wives, including the wife of his best friend and accomplice in these nefarious exploits.

I.15   *bolivar*: A wide-brimmed black silk tophat, named for the South American liberator, much in vogue among liberal thinkers in Petersburg and Paris in the 1820's.

"   *Nevsky Prospect*: The grand axis of Petersburg, along which were situated all the most chic stores and restaurants frequented by Pushkin and his crowd.

"   *Bréguet*: Abraham Louis Bréguet (1747–1823) was a celebrated Swiss-born French watchmaker whose name is seen today, in the company of other greats, in large letters just above the grand arches of the Eiffel Tower.

I.16   *Talón*: A French restaurateur in Petersburg.

"   *Kavérin*: This is Pyotr Pavlovich Kaverin (1794–1855), a swashbuckling cavalier and friend of Pushkin's.

"   *comet wine*: Wine from the 1811 vintage (the year of Halley's comet).

I.17   *Phèdre, Cléopâtre, Moïna*: The female protagonists of dramas, ballets, and operas popular in Pushkin's day. *Phèdre* is a tragedy by Racine, and Moïna is the central character of *Fingal*, a tragedy by Ozerov (see below).

I.18   *Fonvízin*: Denis Ivanovich Fonvizin (1745–1792), poet and playwright well-known for his comedies and satires.

"   *Knyazhnín*: Yakov Borisovich Knyazhnin (1742–1791), author of tragedies and comedies heavily influenced by French contemporaries.

"   *Ózerov*: Vladislav Alexandrovich Ozerov (1769–1816), author of several old-fashioned sentimental tragedies.

"   *Semyónova*: Ekaterina Semyonovna Semyonova, actress famous for her tragic roles, including Shakespeare.

"   *Katénin*: Pavel Alexandrovich Katenin (1792–1853), a friend of Pushkin's, and a translator of Corneille into Russian.

"   *Didelot*: Charles-Louis Didelot (1777–1846), French dancer and choreographer who lived in Petersburg for many years and founded the Russian ballet school.

"   *Shakhovskóy*: Alexander Alexandrovich Shakhovskoy (1777–1846), author of highly successful comedies and satires, some in verse.

Notes

I.19 *Terpsíchore*: In Greek mythology, the muse of Dance.

I.20 *Istómina*: Evdokiya Il'inicha ("Dunyasha") Istomina (1799–1848), a ballerina famous for her pirouettes and for her beauty, which caused more than one fatal duel.

I.24 *the lofty Grimm*: Jean-Jacques Rousseau (1712–1778), the famous Swiss author, philosopher, and champion of nature and liberty, wrote, in his *Confessions,* of watching with repulsion as the French critic and encyclopedist Frédéric Melchior Grimm (1723–1807) cleaned his own fingernails with a brush. Pushkin quotes this passage and pronounces Grimm a prophet in his own times.

I.25 *Chadáyev*: Pyotr Yakovlevich Chadayev (1793–1856), a fop, colonel, Pushkin friend, brilliant free-thinker, and eventually a mystic declared officially insane — mostly for having written (in French) *Lettres philosophiques,* a work that intensified the ongoing sharp debate between pro-Westerners and Slavophiles about Russia's fate.

I.26 *The Slav's Word Guide*: A more literal translation of its title would be "Lexicon of the Russian Academy".

I.32 *Diana, Flora, Elvina*: Ancient Greek goddesses and even more obscure references.

I.33 *Armida*: Sorceress and seductress, heroine of the poem *Jerusalem Delivered* by Torquato Tasso (see note to I.48).

I.35 *Ókhta*: A suburb of Petersburg.

" *vas-is-das*: A transom or a window in a door. The amusing Russian word васисдас phonetically resembles its amusing French counterpart *vasistas,* and both are obviously imitations of the German phrase *Was ist das?* ("What is that?"), although why this phrase is linked to transoms and/or mid-door windows is rather murky.

I.38 *khandrá*: From the same root as our "hypochondria".

" *Childe Harold*: A gloomy, spoiled-rotten, world-weary moper, dreamt up by Byron.

I.42 *Bentham and Say*: Jeremy Bentham (1748–1832), British philosopher and jurist, founder of utilitarianism, and Jean-Baptiste Say (1767–1832), French economist and industrialist of an optimistic and liberal leaning.

" *They suffer sudden surging spleen*: Pushkin's note to this stanza says: "This entire ironic stanza is nothing but a subtle lauding of our beautiful countrywomen. Indeed, it was just in this manner that Boileau, in the guise of a reproach, bestowed highest praise on Louis XIV. Our Russian ladies combine enlightenment, loveliness, and the strictest moral purity with that Oriental charm that so enchanted Madame de Staël." To me, however, Pushkin's note sounds more ironic than the stanza.

I.45 *With Fortune blind, and with men's eyes*: The translator tips his hat to The Bard (check out Sonnet XXIX).

I.48	*Just so, some bard, in verse...*: The author tips his hat to the bard Mikhail Nikitich Muravyov (1757–1807) who, in his poem *To the Goddess of the Neva*, employs similar imagery, but alluding to himself.
"	*droshkies*: Low four-wheeled carriages.
"	*Tasso*: Torquato Tasso (1544–1595), Italian poet famous for writing in a form known as *ottava rima*. His career started out happily but took a turn for the worse, and he eventually was held in an asylum for seven years, after which he wandered in melancholy until his death.
I.49	*Brenta*: North-Italian river that flows from near Trento through the Valsugana into the Adriatic near Venice.
"	*Byron's Albionic lyre*: "Albion" (from Latin *albus*, "white", perhaps referring to the famed white cliffs of Dover and thereabouts) is an old poetic term for England.
"	*Petrarch*: Franceso Petrarca (1304–1374). This Italian humanistic poet wrote with virtuosity in both Latin and Italian, and in his verse he celebrated love, mourned the fragility of existence, and expressed the profound conflict in his soul between mysticism and reason.
I.50	*I stroll the strand...*: "Written in Odessa" (Pushkin's note).
"	*In search of Africa's blue sky...*: On this, Pushkin wrote: "The author, on his mother's side, is of African descent. His ancestor Abram Petrovich Annibal, at eight years of age, was abducted from the shores of Africa and taken to Constantinople, where the Russian ambassador, having rescued him, sent him as a gift to Peter the Great, who baptized him in Vilno. His brother, pursuing him, first went to Constantinople, then to Petersburg, and proposed to buy him back, but Peter I would not agree to return his godchild. Annibal, up till his last years, always remembered Africa, the luxurious life of his father, the nineteen brothers and sisters of whom he was the youngest; he always remembered how they would be led to their father with their hands bound behind their backs, and how he alone was free to swim in the fountains of their home; and he always remembered his beloved sister Lagan, who swam after him, far behind the ship on which he was being carried away. "At eighteen years of age, Annibal was sent by the czar to France, where he began his service in the Regents' Army; he returned to Russia with an injured head and with the rank of a French lieutenant. From that time on he found himself in exclusive service to the Emperor. During the reign of Anna, Annibal, a personal enemy of Bühren, was sent to Siberia under a false pretext. Driven to distraction by loneliness and the bitter climate, he escaped, returned to Petersburg, and revealed himself to his friend Minikh, who was very upset and warned him to hide instantly. Annibal thus

set out for his old estates, where he remained for the duration of Anna's reign; this was counted as service in Siberia. When Elizabeth ascended to the throne, she showered him with kindness. Having retired with the rank of general-in-chief, Annibal died during the reign of Catherine, at the age of 92 years.

"His son, Lieutenant-General Ivan Abramovich Annibal, undeniably merits recognition as one of the most distinguished people in the times of Catherine (he died in 1800).

"In Russia, where the memory of noteworthy people often disappears because of insufficient historical records, the strange life-story of Annibal is known only thanks to family traditions. But we, in time, intend to publish a full biography." [It never happened, alas.]

I.55   *Dolc'è far niente!*: "Sweet it is to do nothing!" in Italian. Note: *Dolc'è* is an iamb, as opposed to the trochaic *dolce*.

I.57   *captives of the wild Salghir*: The Salghir is a river in the Crimea. Pushkin is here alluding to the harem girls in his just-published poem *The Fountain of Bakhchisarai*.

"   *my fair Circassian*: A reference to the Circassian maiden around whom swirls the plot of Pushkin's just-published poem *Captive of the Caucusus*.

Chapter II

epigraph   The quotation from Horace means, roughly, "O rural life!", while the lower phrase is a bilingual play on words, meaning in Russian, "O Russia!" (using an obsolete poetic name for Russia). And in English, even the middle line, "Horace", echoes the other two.

II.14   *featherless bipedal creatures*: The translator tips his hat to Aristotle, who characterized human beings in this strange manner. (Pushkin refers to two-leggedness but not to featherlessness.)

II.22   *childhood/wild wood*: When I came up with this rhyme, I thought it was an ingenious, idiosyncratic find of mine, but then I discovered the exact same rhyme in Charles Johnston's 1977 translation.

II.24   *names that others might find stale*: Pushkin adds the following note here: "Sweet-sounding Greek names, such as 'Agafon', 'Filat', 'Fedora', 'Fyokla', and so forth, are used in our land only by simple people."

II.29   *authors like Rousseau and Richardson*: English novelist Samuel Richardson (1689–1761), though little known today, had an enormous influence throughout Europe in the eighteenth century. Among his novels were *Pamela, or Virtue Rewarded*; *Clarissa Harlowe*; and *The Story of Sir Charles Grandison*. The first two of these were epistolary novels, and the latter two were seven volumes apiece. Much of his writing reflected a feminine point of view, although Grandison was an ideal, sentimental, masculine figure. Richardson's influence is felt clearly in the later novels *Julie, ou La Nouvelle Héloïse* (1761) by Jean-Jacques Rousseau (see the note to stanza I.24) and *The Sufferings of Young Werther* (1774) by Goethe.

II.30   *Lovelace*: Lovelace, a scoundrel with quite incorrigible womanizing tendencies, is the hero of Richardson's novel *Clarissa Harlowe*.

"   *Grandison*: Charles Grandison, Richardson's exemplary masculine hero is, in stark contrast to Lovelace, full of virtue, principle, piety, and other boring qualities.

II.31   *Thus habit from on high's assigned: / It brings no joy, but peace of mind*: In a note, Pushkin here quotes a remark by Chateaubriand (see the notes to IV.26): "Si j'avois la folie de croire encore au bonheur, je le chercherois dans l'habitude." ("Were I so foolish as still to believe in bliss, it would be in habit that I would seek it.")

II.35   *fortune-casting with folksongs*: See the notes to stanza V.8.

"   *buttercup bouquet*: At Trinity (the eighth Sunday after Easter), Russians traditionally atoned for their sins by shedding tears on a bouquet or a birch-tree branch.

"   *rye beer*: A famous Russian concoction known as *kvas*.

II.37   *the Ochákov action*: The Russians' capture, in 1788, of Ochakov, a fortified town on the coast of the Black Sea near Odessa, in the course of a battle with the Turks.

II.38   *All flesh is grass*: The translator's hat-tip to King James.

II.40   *Lethe*: The mythical river of forgetfulness, which flows lethargically through Hades.

Chapter III

epigraph   "She was a girl, she was in love." Jacques Charles Louis de Clinchamp de Malfilâtre (1733–1767), French poet and translator of Virgil into French verse.

III.2   *this Phyllis twin*: Phyllis, in ancient Greek mythology, is a bucolic love goddess.

III.4   *babushka*: This English word, of course borrowed from the Russian *bábushka,* which means "grandmother" and is stressed on its initial syllable, has come to denote a kind of scarf, and, belying its origin, is stressed on its second syllable: "babúshka" (thus in metric accord with "Andryúshka", three lines above).

III.5   *Zhukóvsky's 'sweet Svetlana'*: Pushkin's poet-friend Vasily Andreevich Zhukovsky (1783–1852), who translated, among other poets, Schiller and Homer, wrote a ballad of twenty sonnets called *Svetlana*, in which divining rites portend a fearful destiny, and soon thereafter Svetlana has nightmares about her lover, although in the end she wakes up and all is well.

III.9   *Julie Wolmár*: The heroine of Jean-Jacques Rouseau's above-mentioned novel *Julie, ou La Nouvelle Héloïse*.

"   *Malék-Adhél*: The hero of *Mathilde*, a "mediocre" (if one can rely on Pushkin's judgment) romanesque evocation of the era of the crusades, written by Sophie Risteau Cottin (1770–1807), who also wrote *Malvina* (see V.23).

"   *de Linár*: A character in the autobiographical novel *Valérie* by Barbara Juliane Vietinghoff von Krüdener (1764–1807), a mystical Livonian baroness who was a friend of Madame de Staël (see the note to stanza III.10 and to the epigraph to Chapter IV), and whose writings exercised both a religious and a political influence on Czar Alexander the First.

"   *Young Werther*: Werther is the lovelorn and tormented hero of Goethe's self-revelatory epistolary novel *Die Leiden des Jungen Werthers* (1774), the plot of which (unlike Goethe's own life) ends in suicide.

III.10   *Delphine, Julie, Clarissa*: Delphine is the heroine of the epistolary novel *Delphine* (1802) by Madame de Staël (1766–1817), Julie is the heroine of J.-J. Rousseau's above-mentioned novel *Julie*, and Clarissa is the heroine of Samuel Richardson's above-mentioned seven-volume epistolary novel *Clarissa*.

III.12   *poetic fables by the British*: This stanza refers to several literary works then in vogue, including the novel *The Vampire* (1819) by John Polidori, Byron's physician; *Melmoth the Wanderer* by the Irish writer Charles Robert Maturin (1782–1824), whose Faust-like plot had an influence on Balzac and later on the Surrealists; *The Corsair*, a poem by Byron; *Jean Sbogar*, a novel by Charles Nodier (1780–1844), whose dark, romantic adventure tales lent inspiration to the nineteenth-century French poet Gérard de Nerval and, once again, the Surrealists. The Wandering Jew was a common theme at the time. (It should be borne in mind that these works were not read by young Tatyana; Pushkin is simply mentioning them in a philosophical aside on literary evolution.)

III.13   *Phœbus*: Another name for Apollo, the ancient Greek sun god.

III.22   *"Forego all hope, ye who'd make pass"*: A loose translation of the famous line *Lasciate ogni speranza, voi ch'entrate*, from Dante's *Inferno*. Pushkin includes only the first three words (in Russian).

III.26   *in Cyril's hand*: Two ninth-century brothers, St. Cyril and St. Methodius, devised Glagolitic, an alphabet for writing sacred scriptures in Slavonic; this evolved into what we now call "Cyrillic", the writing system still used for Russian, Bulgarian, and several other languages.

III.27   *Good Intentions*: A slightly more literal translation of the title of the literary–cultural magazine Благонамеренный (*Blagonamérennyj*) is "The Well-Intentioned". All the translators came up with different solutions to this pocket-sized translation problem. Thus Falen says "The Good Samaritan"; Arndt says "The Right-Thinker"; Johnston says "The Well-Meaner"; Elton/Briggs says "The Well-Disposed"; while Deutsch deftly sidesteps the issue, referring simply to "a Moscow magazine".

III.29   *Bogdanóvich*: This is the Ukrainian soldier and poet Ippolit Fyodorovich Bogdanovich (1743–1803), whose most noted work, *Dushenka*, influenced young Pushkin.

"   *Parny*: Évariste Désiré de Forges, Vicomte de Parny (1753–1814) was the author of (among other things) *Poésies érotiques*, a lyrical tribute to feminine grace, and a work that helped usher in the Romantic era in poetry.

III.30   *bard of Feasts*: This is Evgeny Abramovich Baratynsky (1800–1844), who from 1820 to 1824 served in an army regiment in Finland, just as his poem *The Feasts*, a reminiscence of his days of carousing with the Saint Petersburg literary circle, came out. Although Pushkin praised Baratynsky warmly, the latter did not return the compliment, instead describing *Eugene Onegin* as a brilliant but juvenile imitation of Byron.

III.31   *Freischütz*: A romantic opera by Carl Maria von Weber (1786–1826), which had just been launched.

III.33   *Filípievna*: This name, "Filátievna", and "Fadéevna" are three names that Pushkin toyed with for Tatyana's nanny. Of the three, "Filátievna" is probably the most commonly seen in print.

Chapter IV

epigraph   "Morality resides in the nature of things." Jacques Necker (1732–1804), highly regarded and influential Swiss-born French economic leader, theorist, and writer on economic issues; also father of the renowned essayist and novelist Madame de Staël (the Baroness Germaine Necker). This epigraph of Pushkin's was in fact drawn from an essay by Madame de Staël on her father.

IV.1–6   The six opening stanzas of Chapter IV were filled with condescending descriptions of Woman, and Pushkin presumably struck them after he had married, because of the offense they might give his wife, Natalya Nikolaevna Goncharova (1812–1863), described by many as "the most beautiful woman in Moscow".

IV.14   *sweet Hymen*: Hymen was the Greek god of marriage.

IV.17   *"Machinally", to translate badly*: In the original Russian, this line is a parenthetical remark that employs the very new and hence somewhat dubious word машинально (*mashinal'no*), copying the French adverb *machinalement*. On a fairly literal level, the line thus says: "As one says, 'mechanically'". In a sense, Pushkin is translating the French badly into Russian; in a similar sense, I am translating Pushkin's Gallic Russian badly into English.

cherry orchard: Translator's hat-tip to Chekhov. In fact, in the Russian original it says that the pair walked home through vegetable gardens. A little poetic lie-sense.

IV.26 *Chateaubriand*: This is the Viscount François René de Chateaubriand (1768–1848), a moderate monarchist who wrote extensively about revolutions, Christianity, his American travels, history, and politics. His memoirs are noted for their quasi-poetic prose and their lyrical descriptions of nature.

IV.30 *Tolstoy*: This is not the famous novelist (who was still a child when Pushkin died) but Count Fyodor Petrovich Tolstoy (1783–1873), a well-known artist of Pushkin's day, whom Pushkin greatly admired.

" *madrigals*: "Madrigal" in this context means a short love poem, not a piece of choral music.

IV.31 *Yazýkov*: Nikolai Mikhailovich Yazykov (1803–1846), a contemporary lyrical poet and friend of Pushkin.

IV.32 *But quiet!*: Thus Pushkin opens a two-stanza–long mock debate about the merits of classic *odes* (which Pushkin thought of as heavy and old-fashioned), as opposed to the more modern *elegies* (a term for short, meditative lyrics). This mock debate was written as a light-hearted retort to his friend and schoolmate Vil'gel'm Karlovich Kyukhel'beker (1797–1846), who had written an article singing the praises of odes and disparaging elegies.

" *dagger, mask, and horn*: Classic symbols of the stage.

IV.33 *Strange Logic*: This is the satiric poem Чужой Толк (*Chuzhoj Tolk*), whose title is variously translated as "The Other" (Falen), "Meaning Strange" (Elton/Briggs), "As Others See It" (Nabokov), "Others' View" (Johnston), and "Their Views" (Arndt); Deutsch again sidesteps the issue, this time totally. The poem is itself in the form of a four-person debate in which one of the characters — the Author (a.k.a. "glib ode man") — rises to the defense of odes and odists, against the attack of a Critic.

IV.36 This stanza is usually omitted. Nabokov calls it "an exceptionally poor stanza", but I sharply disagree. I thank Jim Falen for providing me with the Russian text.

IV.37 *With Byron's feat in mind*: Byron is reputed to have once swum the Hellespont (a strait that separates the Asian and European parts of Turkey, near Gallipoli and the Dardanelles; it links the Sea of Marmara to the Aegean Sea, and ranges from one to four miles in width).

IV.42 *(You're all supposing... and so I must!)*: The first line of this stanza ends in морозы (*morózy*), the word for "frosts", and lines 3 and 4 say, literally, "The reader is already expecting the rhyme 'розы' [meaning "roses" and pronounced *rózy*]; / And so, take it at once!" Here, of course, Pushkin is playing with the theme of trite, hackneyed "June/moon"-style rhymes, much as he does later on, in stanza VI.44. I was sorely tempted, I must say, on my own line 3, to insert not "rosy" but "розы", in order to rhyme with line 1's "cozy" — but I somehow restrained myself.

IV.43   *Pradt*: Dominique de Pradt (1759–1837), a French political writer. Nabokov in his commentary quotes a wonderful passage from a book Pradt wrote in 1819, in which he observed that in 100 years, the populations of both Russia and the United States would likely reach 100 million each, and that from a military point of view, the two countries resemble each other in that both possess, *dans une très-grande abondance,* one of the most essential elements of warfare — namely, horses!

IV.45   *Perhaps Moët, or Veuve Clicquot*: These are among the most celebrated French wines, while Aÿ, mentioned in the next stanza, is a sparkling champagne produced in the small town of Aÿ, about 120 kilometers east of Paris, just south of Reims. The name is pronounced "ah-*ee*".

IV.50   *Lafontaine*: Not to be confused with the famed French fable writer Jean de la Fontaine, this is the once-famed but now forgotten German novelist August Heinrich Julius Lafontaine (1758–1831), whose "family life" novels were exceedingly popular both in German and in French translation.

Chapter V

epigraph   See the note to stanza III.5.

V.2   *kibítka*: A kind of covered wagon.

V.3   *A rival bard's interpretation...*: Pushkin is here alluding to his friend Prince Vyazemsky's poem *First Snow,* from which the epigraph to Chapter 1 was drawn.

"   *Whose ode paid Finland's maid her due*: And here he is alluding to the epic poem *Edda* by his friend Baratynsky (see the note to III.30).

V.8   *Revealing facts for some poor soul*: There were many methods of divination in those days. One was to throw a piece of molten wax into cold water and then pull it out, interpreting the shape it had congealed into as a sign of what the future holds.

"   *This song from olden times they sing*: Another method was to drop rings into water, then for the assembled group to sing a song, then to pick one ring out and to assign to its owner the fate portended by the song just sung.

"   *"Kitty"*: This song (about two cats sleeping by an oven) was thought to be symbolic of an upcoming wedding, whereas the previous song (about peasants shoveling silver) was taken as ominous of imminent death.

V.9   *There's moon and moon alone, alas*: Yet another method of divination was to somehow foresee an image of one's predestined mate by staring at the moon's reflection.

      "   *Agafón*: And again, one might come to know the name of one's fated husband by asking a random passerby his name. In this case, the name that pops up is one that sounds rather rustic and quaint to the Russian ear.

V.10   *Tatyana planned for divination that night*: One could also attempt to conjure up the spirit of one's fated mate in an all-night séance.

      "   *sad Svetlana's fright*: This again alludes to Zhukovsky's poem *Svetlana* (see the note to III.5), in which, at least in Svetlana's nightmare, her husband-to-be carries her off on horseback to his own grave.

      "   *love-god Lel*: Perhaps the Slavic counterpart to the ancient Greek god Hymen.

V.20   *"She's mine!"*: In the Russian, the last two words of V.19 are "Моё! Моё!", and the first one of V.20 is "Моё!", which makes three consecutive occurrences of one word. This is the only place in the novel where I have noticed a word occurring thrice in a row. Moreover, this is not a random word — leaving aside inflectional changes, it's the very word that both begins and ends the novel — and this rat-a-tat trio of occurrences comes very near the novel's midpoint, to boot. I hasten to add that I seriously doubt that Pushkin did this deliberately, but still, I find it a provocative pattern.

      "   *lays her down upon a small wobbly bench*: Pushkin writes this note here: "One of our critics apparently finds in these verses an impropriety that we do not fathom."

V.22   *Martýn Zadék*: This name appears on various German and Russian dream-interpretation handbooks of the epoch, although most likely it is a pseudonym.

V.23   *Malvina*: A novel by Sophie Risteau Cottin (see the notes to stanza III.9).

      "   *Petriads*: Stories about Peter the Great, recounted in heroic verse.

      "   *Marmontel (Tome III)*: The French writer Jean-François Marmontel (1723–1799) was best known for his moral tales and his novels, which preached tolerance and polemicized against slavery.

V.24   *in alphabetical order*: In the original Russian, a series of nouns in near-alphabetical order is given, but one of them is out of order. What symbolic meaning there was to this exception, only Pushkin knows (or knew).

V.25   *Aurora's crimson fingers*: This echoes a phrase from a poem by the remarkably versatile chemist–poet Mikhail Vasilievich Lomonosov (1711–1765), who, among other accomplishments, founded the University of Moscow in 1755. He wrote books in Latin, French, and Russian, including a history of ancient Russia, a grammar of the

Russian language, a treatise on atmospheric electrical phenomena, an introduction to physical chemistry, a guide to rhetoric, a tome on the nature of light, as well as two tragedies and numerous odes. It is not for nothing that Lomonosov has often been called the "father of modern Russian literature".

"   *britskas*: Somewhat like "czar" (which should be "tsar"), this is a false transcription from the Russian, which is in fact бричка (*brichka*), meaning a light type of carriage.

V.26   *Old portly Pustyakóv*: This surname and all the others in the stanza are deliberately comical. Nabokov suggests English translations for them, as follows: Pustyakov is "Mr. Trifle"; Gvozdin is "Squire Clout"; Skotinin is "Mr. Brutish"; Petushkov is "Young Cockahoop"; Buyanov is "Mr. Rowdy"; and lastly, Flyanov is "Judge Flan".

"   *dear Buyánov*: Vasily Pushkin (1767–1830), the poet's paternal uncle, wrote many poems of which perhaps the best is *The Dangerous Neighbor*, whose hero is named "Buyanov". In this lighthearted and metaphorical sense of relatedness, Buyanov and Pushkin are thus "cousins".

V.27   *Réveillez-vous, belle endormie*: "Awake, beautiful dreamer".

V.32   *Zizí*: This is Evpraksia Nikolaevna Wulf (1809–1883), the youngest daughter of Pushkin's neighbors, the Osipov family, in Mikhailovskoe (where Pushkin lived when banished from Saint Petersburg in the years 1824 to 1826). Pushkin courted nearly every female in the family, but Zizi perhaps the most ardently, when she was twenty or so. She and one of her sisters dined with the poet on the eve of his fatal duel in January, 1837.

V.35   *meadowlands*: The translator tips his hat to the haunting Russian folk song Полюшко Поле (*Polyushko Pole*), in English known as "Meadowlands".

V.40   *all'Albáni*: Francesco Albani (1578–1660), painter from Bologna, famous for his grand, elegiac frescoes.

"   *And from my Notebook Number Five / I'll dump all dumb digressive jive*: Putting these words in Pushkin's mouth is a bit of a stretch, I admit, but the pull was irresistible. In any case, the dense sonic repetition here suggests quite accurately the flavor of the Russian final couplet.

Chapter VI

epigraph   "There, below the brief, cloudy days, / Is born a race whom death does not aggrieve." Petrarch (see notes to stanza I.49).

VI.5   *Old Regulus*: Marcus Atilius Regulus (died ca. 250 B.C.), a Roman general. Captured by the Carthaginians in the First Punic War in roughly 255 B.C., he was held for five years, then sent to Rome to negotiate a surrender; once home, however, he instead argued and persuaded the Roman Senate to continue the war, after which he returned to Carthage, knowing full well that he would have to pay for his decision with his life — and he did.

"   *chez Véry*: An allusion to Véry Frères, a posh Parisian restaurant of the epoch.

VI.7   *Sed alia témpora*: "But time has wings."

"   *acacias and cherries*: Nabokov, in his commentary, flies into a botanicolinguistic paroxysm here, heaping pages of bile and scorn on previous translators' renderings of черёмуха ("a kind of cherry tree", says my dictionary) and акация ("acacia", says my dictionary), and going into all the profound and elusive cultural nuances of these two words (and which, it is tacitly implied, are universal among Russians). After over four pages of ranting, Nabokov winds up revealing to his faithful readers what "the correct way" to translate these words is — namely, as "racemosas and pea trees". Obviously, he would consider my dictionary-lookup methodology of "translation" of tree-names beneath contempt.

"   *Horatius*: Horace's name, in its original Latin form.

VI.10   *un monsieur très distingué*: The translator tips his hat to the golden era of French popular song.

VI.20   *Delvig*: Anton Antonovich Delvig (1798–1831). One of Pushkin's most intimate friends from his halcyon *Lycée* days (see notes to VIII.1), a poet, and the editor of the short-lived poetry journal *Northern Flowers*. Nabokov points out with justified amazement the fact that Delvig, at age sixteen, wrote a lovely 24-line pæan to his fifteen-year-old comrade Pushkin, praising his lyric poetry and prophesying poetic immortality for his friend. Nabokov (who is not *all* bad!) gives a literal gloss of the poem in English and touchingly adds, "This is a combination of intuitive genius and actual destiny to which I can find no parallel in the history of world poetry."

VI.21   *His lines by luck were kept; let's scan some*: In Chapter 9 of *Le Ton beau de Marot*, I refer to Nabokov's commentary on this stanza, for it turns out that he quotes a Clément Marot poem as evidence that Pushkin was borrowing, consciously or unconsciously, from then-current Gallic poetic vogues. Since the Marot poem expresses ideas most similar to those in Lensky's poem, my first four lines of Lensky's poetic outburst are taken almost word for word from my translation of the Marot in my book.

"   *Tomorrow's clement*: Note the phonetics of these words.

VI.24   *Phosphor*: Pushkin writes Веспер here, which is the Russian for "Hesper", meaning "the evening star", when what he in fact means to be referring to is the *morning* star ("Phosphor"). I have thus taken the liberty of correcting this small error. On the other hand, since the morning star *equals* the evening star (both are the planet Venus), philosophers might chide me, either for making the substitution or for claiming Pushkin erred.

VI.25   *To load Lepage*: Jean Lepage (1779–1822) was a famous Parisian gunsmith.

VI.26   *excuses/the deuce is*: Another of those rhymes I felt so proud of, but when I looked at Elton's 1936 version, there it was, staring up at me, anticipating me by over sixty years!

VI.32   *To moon is odd*: Тому назад одно мгновенье... (*Tomú nazád odnó mgnovén'e...* — Only one moment ago...)

VI.36   *Still sacred to Vladímir's ghost*: Yes, but which Vladimir?

VI.44   *O dreams, o dreams, where's all your sweetness? / Your flower's fled with — trite rhyme — "fleetness"*: The lines in Russian here involve the rhyme of сладость (*sládost'* — "sweetness") and младость (*mládost'* — "youth"), which Pushkin calls an "eternal rhyme". I strove here to find an "eternal" (*i.e.*, trite) English rhyme both of whose words connected with Pushkin's words, in terms of their semantics. To buttress my calling this rhyme "trite", I would point out that it does in fact appear elsewhere in my translation — namely, in IV.11.

Chapter VII

epigraphs   Ivan Ivanovich Dmitriev (1760–1837), was an author of fables, songs, tales, and in this case, the poem *The Liberation of Moscow*. As for Baratynsky, see the notes to III.30. The playwright Alexander Sergeevich Griboedov (1795–1829) was one of Russia's great early literary voices, but his voice was tragically stilled when he was assassinated while serving as Russian ambassador to Persia. This brief exchange is from his best-known play, Горе от Ума (*Woe from Wit*), dating from 1824.

VII.2   *Lévshin's school of reason*: Vasily Levshin (1746–1826) was a prolific author of both fiction and nonfiction. Among other things he was an authority on flower gardens and vegetable gardens, and through his prolific writings he taught about windmills, watermills, and many other aspects of rural life. There seems to be disagreement about whether his last name is Левшин (*Levshin*) or Лёвшин (*Lyovshin*). I opt for the former, perhaps because Nabokov opts for the latter.

VII.10   *uhlan*: This means "lancer".

VII.18   *durachkí*: A children's card game.

VII.22   *Don Juan's bard*: This refers to Byron (and though the British insist on their "Don *Joo*-an", I say "Don Hwan").

VII.35   *Like spaced-out fenceposts flashing by*: In a note, Pushkin quotes a mysterious personage "K" as saying that, when sent as an envoy from the Prince to the Empress, he had stuck his sword out the carriage window and the verstposts rushed by so fast that it seemed as if his sword were banging against a picket fence.

VII.38   *gold clocks*: In this long list of items seen in Moscow's lively streets, I took the slight liberty of adding just one that Pushkin did not mention: "gold clocks". It seems so clearly to mesh neatly with all the rest of the scene that Pushkin is painting that I felt no guilt at so doing. This was a typical use of poetic lie-sense.

VII.45   *Herr Kleinmaus*: Another example of poetic lie-sense was my substitution of German "Herr Kleinmaus" for French мосьё Финмуш ("monsieur Finemouche").

"   *for three*: And in this closing line, for the sake of rhyme, I had the gall to change "two" into "three". For Nabokov, this would be an unforgivable sin.

VII.49   *Strutting youths in cushy government jobs*: This alludes to wealthy young layabouts who were often given sinecures in the Foreign Affairs Ministry's Archive Department.

"   *Friend Vyázemsky*: Pushkin loves inserting his friends into his tale. See also my note to the epigraph to Chapter One.

VII.50   *Muse Melpómene*: The three muses mentioned here are Melpomene (the muse of song, harmony, and tragedy), Thalia (the muse of comedy and light poetry), and Terpsichore (the muse of dance, dramatic chorus, and lyric poetry).

VII.51   *To the Sobránie*: This was officially called the "Russian Assembly of Nobility".

VII.55   *On whom three words now (plus three dozen)*: Here Pushkin says, fairly sloppily, "about whom two words now"; my counting, luckily, is more exact than our bard's.

"   *my hat/that's that*: Yet another original rhyme on which I congratulated myself — and then found the same rhyme in the same place, in a far earlier edition. In this case, it was Babette Deutsch who scooped me, all the way back in 1937. Shucks!

Chapter VIII

epigraph   Taken from *Fare Thee Well*, a poem Byron addressed to his wife, from whom separation was growing inevitable.

VIII.1   *au Lycée*: This was the лицей, the elite boarding school in the town of Tsarskoe Selo (which was renamed "Pushkin" around 80 years ago), where Pushkin spent his adolescence from 1811 to 1817, where he made lifelong close friends, and where he began writing poetry. The лицей was joined to the "Catherine Palace", one of the most beautiful and grand of all Russia's palaces (reduced to rubble in World War II yet now rebuilt, at unimaginable cost and effort). I have heard it said that Pushkin wrote over 100 poems celebrating his years in the лицей.

VIII.2   *Derzhávin*: A major figure of Russian literature of the
eighteenth century, Gavrila Romanovich Derzhavin
(1743–1816) was primarily a poet and a rather daring
one at that, anticipating many later tendencies. As this
stanza says, he visited the лицей and there, in early
1815, he heard Pushkin recite a poem he had just
composed. Derzhavin liked Pushkin's style and gave
the lad his blessing, which Pushkin never forgot.

"   *"And Dmítriev, too, endured my lays" (Pope)*: Usually just
the first four lines of VIII.2 are printed, but my Russian
EO edition gives them all, so I chose to translate the
whole stanza. As to this particular line of it, Nabokov,
ever diligent, has done the scholarly spadework and
discovered that Pushkin, in order to tip his hat to old
Dmitriev, borrowed a line from Dmitriev's own Russian
translation of Alexander Pope's 1734 poem *Epistle to Dr.
Arbuthnot.* But then it turns out that Dmitriev, knowing
no English, had translated this English poem to Russian
from a French translation! So far so good. But then
Nabokov quotes to us the original line in Pope's poem
(which then passed via French and Dmitriev to Pushkin
and was "tweaked" by Pushkin so that Dmitriev's name
appeared instead of Swift's), and it is this: "and Swift
endur'd my Lays". So Nabokov muses, "I submit that,
in an accurate English translation…. we should resist
the formidable temptation to render Pushkin's line:
'And Dmitriev, too, endured my lays'." But yours truly,
given this formidable temptation, simply couldn't resist.
However, I instantly noticed that Nabokov's devilish
little idea won't work because, as he well knew, line 5 of
any Onegin stanza has got to be feminine. This led to
my adding the parenthesized attribution at the end.

"   *Karamzín*: Nikolai Karamzin (1766–1826) was a truly
pivotal figure in the evolution of Russian literature, and
Pushkin, like all later writers, owed him a giant debt. It
was Karamzin who, in his twenties, decided to express
himself in contemporary-style Russian rather than in an
antiquated, artificial Russian that was deeply redolent
of Old Church Slavonic, yet which, in his day, was the
standard for all writing. Having shucked these tight old
shackles, Karamzin then embraced the muse and went
on to write many poems, short stories, and novels in a
modernized, streamlined, "lite" Russian that caught on
like wildfire among other writers (and, needless to say,
among readers!). His sentimental short story *Poor Liza*
(1792) knew great success (a Gallicism), but his most
lasting contribution (other than his reformist views)
was his monumental twelve-volume *History of the Russian
State,* published between 1816 and 1829.

"   *Zhukóvsky*: Vasily Zhukovsky (see notes to stanza III.5),
Pushkin's friend and mentor, welcomed Karamzin's
new-fangled Russian and wielded it gracefully in his
own verse as well as in his verse translations of verse
(which Nabokov, for some reason, hesitates to bash,

despite the fact that he mercilessly bashes everyone else's verse-to-verse translations).

VIII.4   *Lenore*: This is the heroine of a famous ballad by the German poet Gottfried August Bürger (1747–1794). Lenore is spirited off by her lover on his strong steed and then, mounted together in moonlight, they gallop away over hill and through dale, headed for their nuptial bed, which, however, turns out to be his grave.

"   *Tauris*: An ancient name for the Crimea.

"   *Nereids*: These sea nymphs, fifty in number, were the daughters of the sea god Nereus.

VIII.12   *my Demon*: This is an allusion to Pushkin's 1823 poem *My Demon* (later renamed simply "Demon"), in which the poet is visited by a deeply troubling Spirit of Doubt.

VIII.13   *from deck to dance*: Chatsky, a character in Griboedov's play *Woe from Wit* (see notes to the epigraph of Chapter VII), has been on a three-year voyage to points west, including France, and one evening turns up, out of the blue, back in old Moscow town and jauntily bounces, as Pushkin puts it, с корабля на бал (*s korablyá na bal*): "from boat to ball". Nabokov, however, terms Chatsky's nonchalant bounce a "transition from deck to dance". There's little else I need explain.

VIII.14   *Shishkóv*: Admiral Alexander S. Shishkov (1754–1841) was a reactionary author and member of the "Archaics", who gained great notoriety for his bitter attacks on the use of foreign words in Russian. Nabokov proudly points out that he and Shishkov are distantly related.

VIII.16   *In epigrams, it might be splendid*: The English word "vulgar" is close enough, phonetically, to the Russian last name "Bulgarin" that Pushkin can dream, it seems, of using the word in an epigram aimed at tweaking Faddei Bulgarin (1789–1859), literary critic and police informer, between Pushkin and whom no love was lost.

"   *Nina Voronskáya*: Nina Voronskaya seems to be a hypothetical heartbreaker, an imaginary composite of various Petersburg society belles of the time.

VIII.21   *Prince N*: In Tchaikovsky's opera *Eugene Onegin*, Prince N is, for some reason, renamed "Prince Gremin".

VIII.26   *Prolásov*: This is not an allusion to any specific person; the name simply exudes, to a Russian ear, connotations of "sycophant" or "social climber".

"   *Saint-Priest*: Emmanuil Sen-Pri (1806–1828), a talented and well-known half-French caricaturist of the times.

VIII.35   *Manzoni, Fontenelle, Chamfort*: Some quick notes on this motley collection of thinkers and writers... Alessandro Manzoni (1785–1873), Italian novelist who shot to stardom for *I Promessi Sposi*, which had just appeared in 1827; Bernard Le Bovier de Fontenelle (1657–1757),

French poet, *bon vivant,* philosopher, and scientific popularizer; Sébastien Roch Nicolas de Chamfort (1741–1794), French moralist and sympathizer to the Revolution, but opponent of violence, best known for his caustic epigrams and witty fables; Edward Gibbon (1737–1794), English historian, author of *The Decline and Fall of the Roman Empire* (1776); Jean-Jacques Rousseau (see notes to stanzas I.24 and II.29); Johann Gottfried Herder (1744–1803), German writer and philosopher who championed the wisdom of the common people and thereby influenced Goethe and the *Sturm und Drang* movement; Madame de Staël (pronounced like the French word *stalle*; see notes to stanza III.10 and to the epigraph to Chapter IV); Pierre Bayle (rhymes with the French word *belle*) (1647–1706), French historian and philosopher of religion and morality who, through his well-reasoned and erudite criticisms of authoritarian religion and his advocacy of tolerance, exerted considerable influence on the philosophers of the eighteenth century; Tissot — now there is a question mark here, for there are two Tissots: Simon André (or possibly "Samuel Auguste") Tissot (1728–1797), Swiss doctor and author of *De la santé des gens de lettres,* and Pierre François Tissot (1768–1854), French historian and author of *De la poésie latine* — so reader, take your pick; and lastly, Marie François Xavier Bichat (1771–1802), French anatomist and physiologist.

Whereas I felt free to introduce "gold clocks" into the list of items seen on Moscow's busy streets in VII.38, I certainly would not have felt free to introduce other authors into this list (or to delete any). But why exactly is that the case?

" *È sempre bene*: "It's always fine."

VIII.38 *Benedetta... or Idol Mio*: Two Italian songs popular at the time. *Benedetta sia la madre* is a Venetian barcarolle, and *Idol mio* is the opening pair of words of a refrain in a duettino by Vincenzo Gabussi (1800–1846).

VIII.51 *as once Saadi said*: Musli-ud-Din Saadi (sometimes spelled "Sa'di") was a Persian poet who lived in the environs of Shiraz from roughly 1200 till roughly 1291. He wrote many love poems, and his *Gulistân,* translated into French in 1634, was the first work of Persian poetry known in the West. These lines, attributed by Pushkin to Saadi, have not been found in the poet's writings, but in any case they are said to reflect Pushkin's nostalgia at the dwindling of his own circle of friends, of whom at least some were among the ill-fated band of revolutionaries known as the "Decembrists", who, after their failed revolt of 1825, were captured and exiled to Siberia, where many died.

•

Bibliography

Edmonds, Robin (1994). *Pushkin: The Man and His Age.* New York: St. Martin's Press.

Hofstadter, Douglas R. (1996). "What's Gained in Translation". *New York Times Book Review,* December 8.

—— (1997). *Le Ton beau de Marot: In Praise of the Music of Language.* New York: Basic Books.

Katzner, Kenneth (1994). *English–Russian and Russian–English Dictionary.* New York: John Wiley & Sons.

Nabokov, Vladimir (1990). *Strong Opinions.* [1973] New York: Vintage Books.

Pushkin, Alexander (1991). *Евгений Онегин.* [1831] In Russian. London: Bristol Classical Press.

—— (1943). *Eugene Onegin.* Translated by Babette Deutsch. New York: Heritage Press. Reissued by Dover Publications, 1999.

—— (1977). *Eugene Onegin.* Translated by Charles Johnston. London: Penguin Books.

—— (1980). *Eugène Oniéguine.* Translated by Maurice Colin. Paris: Université de Dijon/Société «Les belles lettres».

—— (1981). *Eugen Onegin.* Translated by Ulrich Busch. Zürich: Manesse Verlag.

—— (1984). *Jewgenij Onegin.* Translated by Rolf-Dietrich Keil. Giessen: W. Schmitz Verlag.

—— (1990). *Eugene Onegin: A Novel in Verse.* [1964] Translated by Vladimir Nabokov. Volume I: Introduction and Translation; Volume II: Commentary and Index. Princeton, New Jersey: Princeton University Press.

—— (1990). *Eugene Onegin.* Translated by James E. Falen. Carbondale, Illinois: Southern Illinois University Press. Reissued by Oxford University Press, 1995.

—— (1992). *Eugene Onegin.* Translated by Walter Arndt. [1963] Ann Arbor, Michigan: Ardis Editions.

—— (1995). *Yevgeny Onegin.* Translated by Oliver Elton [1937]; edited and revised by A. D. P. Briggs. London: J. M. Dent.

Robert, Paul (1974). *Le Petit Robert 2: Dictionnaire universel des noms propres.* Paris: S.E.P.R.E.T.

Seth, Vikram (1986). *The Golden Gate.* New York: Random House.

Weaver, Warren (1955). "Translation". In W. N. Locke and A. D. Booth (eds.), *Machine Translation of Languages* (MIT Press, Cambridge, Massachusetts).

Wilson, Edmund (1965). Review of Nabokov's translation of *Eugene Onegin. New York Review of Books,* July 15. Also in Edmund Wilson, *A Window on Russia* (Farrar, Straus & Giroux, New York, 1972).

Permissions

*Grateful acknowledgment is made by the author to the
following individuals and publishers for permission to quote
from the sources indicated. Every effort has been made to
locate the copyright owners of material reproduced in this
book. Any errors or omissions that are brought to the
author's attention will be corrected in subsequent printings.*

•

Words of Thanks

MY UNCLE Jimmy Givan, when a teen-ager growing up in Baltimore in the twenties and thirties, was caught up, as were so many people, old and young, in the then-magical world of the American popular song, and, inspired by the likes of Cole Porter and Ira Gershwin, he wrote clever lyrics to tunes by his friend Roy. Jimmy's deft verbal touch resonated with his younger sister Nancy, who was developing her own deep love for words and how they can work together in musical ways; she, in turn, when she became my mother, passed this love on to me when I was too young to appreciate what I was absorbing osmotically. It is thus to her, more than to anyone else, that I owe my passion for seeking the *mot juste,* for savoring the occasional *bon mot,* and for trying out endless variations on every last little turn of phrase — ironically, a trait of mine that drives her batty when I run them by her.

In 1986, my mother gave me Vikram Seth's novel in verse *The Golden Gate,* my instant resonance with which launched my life down new pathways. Among other things, Seth's book served as my introduction to Pushkin's *Eugene Onegin.* It was some years later that, in unforgettable sessions of reading aloud with my late wife Carol, I fell in love with this wondrous work as lyrically anglicized by James Falen. Eventually I came across several other translations of *Eugene Onegin,* and in 1995 I was encouraged by Carolyn Rand Herron of *The New York Times Book Review* to write an essay commenting on four of them. The careful comparison that I carried out in order to write that essay brought me closer and closer to the original Russian text, but I still resisted tackling it, assuming it to be far beyond my ability to follow.

Finally in 1997, inspired by words of my Russian friend Marina Eskina, I took the bull by the horns and started reading and then memorizing bits — at first small, but eventually quite sizable — of the original Pushkin. In those early stages, another Russian friend, Ariadna Solovyova, gave me much help as I was starting my trek up the mysterious, alluring slopes of Russian pronunciation. Subsequently, several other native speakers of Russian — Larisa Migachyov, Katya Stesina, Oksana Gill, Katya Vernikova, and Julia Trubikhina — helped me in my pursuit of their language and in understanding various fine points of one stanza or another.

Thanks to Rima Greenhill and Lazar Fleishman of Stanford's Slavic Languages Department, I was invited in late 1997 to a banquet in honor of Alexander Pushkin at which I had the special luck and honor of meeting Kenneth Pushkin, founder of The Pushkin Legacy, devoted to commemorating the bicentennial year of Kenneth's namesake and relative. Although they probably did not suspect anything of the kind, Rima, Lazar, and Kenneth, with their warm and spontaneous encouragement of my unusual mode of involvement with *Eugene Onegin,* helped catalyze the transmutation of my first playful dabblings in the waters of *Onegin* translation into a deeper (though still playful) immersion.

My next debt — and one that truly cannot be overestimated — is to those who have preceded me as translators of *Evgenij Onegin* into verse in English and other languages, most notably Babette Deutsch, Oliver Elton, A. D. P. Briggs, Walter Arndt, Charles Johnston, James Falen, Maurice Colin, Ulrich Busch, and Rolf-Dietrich Keil. Along with them I would even include Vladimir Nabokov, whose devotion to Pushkin's glowing poetic voice matches that of anyone, but whose nebulous philosophy of translation remains utterly unpersuasive to me, much as his implacably bitter attitude towards his rivals remains, in my mind, an exemplary monument to the frailty of the human ego.

I am very grateful to John Donatich of Basic Books, whose open-mindedness as a publisher is symbolized by his willingness to come out with an English-language *Onegin* issuing from the pen of someone whose credentials as a Russian speaker are essentially nil. Speaking of my dubious level of Russian, I would like to mention the individual who, many years ago, gave me my very first intense exposure to the Russian language, when we were both graduate students at the University of Oregon: Ron Goodwin. I still vividly remember auditing Ron's second-year Russian course and admiring his fluent command and his wonderful accent.

Here at Indiana University, I have enjoyed the warm support of a large number of colleagues, but I must single out for special mention Helga Keller, Howard Keller, Mort Lowengrub, Willis Barnstone, and Matei Calinescu.

As anyone who flips through this book can see, I owe Achille Varzi many thanks for his subtle, sensitive, and charming sketches that grace the ends of all the chapters, as well as the cover.

For having organized or having been otherwise involved in my memorable visit to St. Petersburg in October of 1998, I would like to thank Kenneth Pushkin, Galina Sergeeva, Irina Molozina, Yuliya Korn, and Sergei Nekrasov.

Deeply appreciated warmth during this time has come from people in many quarters, including Tim Wiles and Mary McGann, Marilyn Stone, Sue Wunder, Inga Karliner, Scott Buresh, Robert Boeninger, my sister Laura Hofstadter, Charles Brenner, Patrizia Weber, Raffaella Bertagnolli, Federica Vulcan, Lucia Dell'Eva and Franco Groaz, Barbara Wolf, Jeff and Elinor Favinger, Oliviero Stock, Vassil Nikolov, Steve and Aleka Blackwell, Steve and Cindy Howard, Kellie O'Connor Gutman — and finally but foremost, a flowery flourish of the proverbial hat to Greg Huber for his wit and his insight, his companionship, and his generosity of spirit.

From its start, Jim and Eve Falen have been warm supporters of my quixotic effort, and out of our common admiration of the same great work of art, we have forged a solid friendship.

My children, Danny (10 as I write) and Monica (7), have had to put up with Daddy's latest crazy obsession for over a year now, and they have never complained once. *Grazie molte, bimbi!*

A striking irony about this anglicization of Russia's most classic poem is that its translator remains woefully ignorant about the bulk of Russian literature — even about the majority of Pushkin's own output. It is, however, my fond hope that, with *Eugene Onegin* serving as my entry point, I will proceed, in the years to come, to explore the famously rich veins of Russian prose and poetry that, in carrying out this labor of love, I have only begun to mine.

Words of Thanks